Praise for *Robert's Rules of Innovation II:*
The Art of Implementation

"Robert Brands's book stands out as one written by someone who understands the harsh reality of making innovation work in corporate environments, from his own experience. He provides personal insights for the whole journey, from igniting creativity to convincing stubborn management, from crowdsourcing new ideas to getting the most out of different generations in your team. It's a great read for those embarking on this journey for the first time, as well as for hardened professionals who want to confirm they're on the right track. Because successfully innovating is difficult and sometimes defies logic; yet Robert packs the essence into this excellent book."
—Costas Papaikonomou, cofounder, Happen Group

"What a delight to experience a book that balances theory and practice in the pursuit of innovation. *Robert's Rules of Innovation II: The Art of Implementation* delivers on its promise of providing thought leaders, practitioners, and global change leaders with impactful ideas for introducing and implementing innovation excellence in a reinvented world."
—Dee McCrorey, author of *Innovation in a Reinvented World: 10 Essential Elements to Succeed in the New World of Business*

"Lightning strikes again for Robert Brands with his second book, *Robert's Rules of Innovation II: The Art of Implementation*. Robert picks up, in a seamless way, where he left off in his first book to give the reader a step-by-step approach to successfully implementing a culture of innovation within their organization. His words are clear. His process is proven, and his message is critical. If you're a CEO, business leader or C-suite executive you need to read this book and keep it in a prominent spot on your desk where you can easily reach for it."
—Chris Ruisi, executive leadership expert and author of *Step Up and Play Big: Unlock Your Potential to Be Exceptional in 8 Simple Steps*

Praise for *Robert's Rules of Innovation* (Wiley, 2010)

"One surefire way to develop a compelling competitive advantage is through innovation. Every company needs this well-crafted blueprint to innovation success."
—Jaynie Smith, author of, *Creating Competitive Advantage* and President of, Smart Advantage, Inc.

"I like *Robert's Rules* because it provides practical guidelines for ensuring successful innovation. The author's vast experience with innovation projects provides context for understanding the challenges innovators are facing and how they can be overcome to become successful innovators."
—Han Gerrits, CEO, of Innovation Factory and professor, at Vrije Universiteit, Amsterdam

"I hate rule books. But I love *Robert's Rules of Innovation*. This highly practical book, with its hands-on advice and detailed guidelines, is guaranteed to help you turn innovation from the enigmatic into the systematic."
—Rowan Gibson, coauthor, *Innovation to the Core*

"Innovation: Easy to talk about, hard to execute. Robert Brands teaches us not only how to create the conditions in which innovation occurs, but how to verify that we've done our job at each stage. No business can truly compete without vibrant innovation. *Robert's Rules of Innovation* shows us how to get there and—most important—how to be consistent at it. Highly recommended."
—Peter Firestein, author, *Crisis of Character: Building Corporate Reputation in the Age of Skepticism*

"As corporations understand more and more that consumers own brands, *Robert's Rules of Innovation* brings the road map on how to deliver the new ideas people want to the marketplace."
—Marc Gobe, President of Emotional Branding, LLC, and bestselling author of *Emotional Branding*

ROBERT'S RULES
OF
INNOVATION II

The Art of Implementation

ROBERT F. BRANDS
with Martin Kleinman

BASCOM HILL PUBLISHING GROUP • MINNEAPOLIS, MN

BASCOM HILL
PUBLISHING GROUP

Copyright © 2015 by Brands & Company, LLC

Bascom Hill Publishing Group
322 First Avenue N, 5th floor
Minneapolis, MN 55401
612.455.2294
www.bascomhillbooks.com

ISBN-13: 978-1-63413-730-0
LCCN: 2015912870

Distributed by Itasca Books

Cover Design by THCreativity, Inc.
Typeset by B. Cook

Printed in the United States of America

I dedicated my first book to my grandfather, whom I looked up to and who inspired me. This second book is dedicated to my father and to my sons, Alex and Eric, who are continuing the family's entrepreneurial lineage.

Contents

Introduction

Innovation is the key to your company's survival. And mastery of the **art of implementation** ensures that your innovation program clicks on all cylinders, all the time.

Before we begin our new journey together, let's take a quick trip in the time machine back to 2008–2009. As our first book was being written, the global economy was in the throes of the deepest and broadest economic crisis since the Great Depression.

Short memories are human nature. But I vividly recall, all too well, dim days such as September 29, 2008, when the Dow Jones Industrial Average plummeted 777.68 points. It was the biggest one-day drop in the history of the Dow, and the largest percentage decline since trading resumed following the 9/11 terrorist attacks.

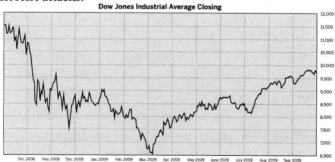

Source THCreativity, Inc.

That fall, the business landscape was transformed. Business owners froze, hiring stopped, firing began. Business investment dried up. R&D programs were put on ice, and sometimes gutted completely. Many otherwise savvy managers instituted an "addition by subtraction" mentality and began to cut, cut, cut—way past the fat and into the very bone of their organizations.

"Batten down the hatches, folks, and prepare to weather the storm." The prevailing attitude was a mind-set ruled by fear, although we know—intellectually—that cutting innovation and R&D during a downturn is the worst course of action.

Bear in mind that this mentality came on the heels of years of "leaning out operations." The idea was to improve efficiencies and maximize profits. But, given the scenario, there was little left to give, operationally speaking. Yet, in the face of the overwhelming economic catastrophe in the late 2000s, this is exactly the direction many people took.

As this second *Robert's Rules of Innovation* book is being written in 2014, five years since the "end" of the Great Recession, metrics indicate that the US has regained the nine million jobs shed. The Dow Jones Industrial Average has recovered from its losses, and more recently it has been dancing above the seventeen-thousand-point mark. On paper, at least, one would assume that times are incrementally better.

Yes and no. Balance sheets look strong and many large corporations are awash in cash. M&A activity is red-hot.

And yet today's consumers are uneasy, and for good reason. Wages remain stagnant, adjusted for inflation. Millions of working-age people now compete for virtually the same number of jobs that existed in 2008. Previously, when you received your degree you were practically guaranteed a job. Not so anymore. Underemployment is still a serious problem, and the millennial generation—our future—is having a tough time gaining a toehold in professional life.

As a leader of multinational companies, as well as a consultant working with top executives in both the public and private sector, I see a repeated failure of **innovation implementation**. I can recall the great prerecession intentions regarding renewed emphasis on innovation. However, after the storms of the late 2000s, those intentions have vanished in the mist, lost at sea.

Today, the business leaders I meet with still keep a white-knuckled death grip on overhead, despite the vastly improved health of their balance sheets and order banks. Disturbingly, this includes new product development programs.

My name is Robert Brands. I was born and raised in The Netherlands. My father, an entrepreneur in his own right, who still lives in The Netherlands, remains a great influence in my life, and we talk regularly about the state of business today. In his opinion, this continued reluctance to recommit to innovation is reminiscent of the financial behavior of those who lived through the Great Depression of the 1930s. Back then, he says, the line between prudent thrift and counterproductive cost slashing became blurred—even as the economy improved. The cautiousness of the Depression generation continued for decades, he notes. Many individuals who lived through the toughest times and later became affluent and successful refused to loosen their grip and let out the reins, financially speaking.

The fear instilled by those horrific days long ago became permanently imprinted on business behavior patterns.

Do you know anyone who takes that kind of tight-fisted approach to R&D and innovation, as if we were still in the roiling financial tumult of 2008?

I do.

I have led innovation-driven companies around the world, and the business leaders in my global network differ in many ways. We come from different cultures, speak different languages, and are experts across a variety of industries.

But together we share a passion for innovation and the art of implementation. It's one thing to want, plan, and encourage a culture of innovation. It's quite another thing to commit the time, energy, and resources to implement this innovation process and to make sure it is permanently encoded in your organization's genetic material.

In the first book, we delineated decades' worth of collective invaluable experience. *Robert's Rules of Innovation*—much like *Robert's Rules of Order*, which create order from chaos in meetings around the world—helped business leaders understand the principles needed to create, nurture, and profit from a stable new product development (NPD) program.

With *The Art of Implementation*, we will quickly revisit the ten key rules of innovation and then dive headfirst into practical techniques to break down the barriers to innovation, whether they are self-imposed or due to external or marketplace reasons.

As with our first book, *The Art of Implementation* will take a hands-on, understandable, and practical approach to making innovation part of your outfit's DNA.

In this second volume, you will note that the topics naturally fall into three distinct areas:

- "Big Ideas"
- The "People Aspects" of Implementation
- The "Process" of Implementation

Rotating these three broad content areas will keep things interesting as you read, as it helps you map an implementation plan for your own organization.

The worst of the Great Recession is long over. There are no more excuses, no more reasons to postpone, defund, ignore, or otherwise hobble your NPD programs. Because, let's face it, whether you manage a multinational business or an entrepreneurial start-up, whether you are a manufacturer, distributor, service provider, supplier, or retailer, the competitive pressures today—in terms of time, budget, *everything*—are unprecedented in our lifetimes.

There is no time to waste.

So let me introduce you to the best and most recent thinking of my international network of innovators. Together we will show you how to permanently implement a culture of innovation in your work environment.

Ready to unleash your team's abilities? Eager to make sure your culture of innovation is properly implemented, so that you are poised to create profitable new products and position your company for long-term success?

Welcome, then, to ***Robert's Rules of Innovation II: The Art of Implementation.***

Create Your Innovation Mantra

"It's impossible," said Pride.
"It's risky," said Experience.
"It's pointless," said Reason.
"Give it a try," whispered the Heart.
—Unknown

Robert's Rules of Innovation II: The Art of Implementation is your road map for success through innovation. In these pages, you will learn the elements that must be in place to properly execute the ten imperatives to innovation discussed in detail in our first book.

In fact, before we delve into specifics, it will be advantageous to recap each of the ten **Robert's Rules of Innovation (RROI)** set forth in our first book, *Robert's Rules of Innovation: A 10-Step Program for Corporate Survival.*

Review Class: Robert's Rules of Innovation Revisited

Robert's Rules of Innovation are the ten steps you need to follow in order to deliver profitable growth through **I-n-n-o-v-a-t-i-o-n**.

We go from the "I" of *Inspiration* to the "N" of *Net Results* and address all the parameters needed for a long-term, enduring, and successful innovation strategy that is both profitable and repeatable.

Bear in mind, these are "rules of order"—for innovation requires rules to enable your innovation program to succeed.

And what are those rules?

- **I**nspire/Initiate
- **N**o Risk, No Innovation
- **N**ew Product Development Process
- **O**wnership
- **V**alue Creation
- **A**ccountability
- **T**raining and Coaching
- **I**dea Management
- **O**bserve and Measure
- **N**et Result and Reward

- **Inspire/Initiate**

The leader of the NPD effort, your innovation SWAT team, has to inspire, lead, and *drive* the process. It has to come from the top, and the effort has to be an integral part of your company's culture. This is an imperative.

When innovation efforts fail, the culprit is usually culture or people-related issues. It can't be a "flavor of the month" effort. For the NPD program to work, the leader—in any company, that person has to be the CEO—has to be regularly and personally involved, so that everyone understands *this is the way it's going to be*. It's all about accountability and good-natured shepherding. The leader needs to ensure that project-by-project timelines and investment decisions are on-track. He or she has to be the chief innovation officer.

The takeaway? A new culture is developed, one that runs throughout the organization. Do it right, step-by-step, building consensus, reinforcing ideas, and underscoring the need for accountability. Don't rush it, but don't waver either. Remain consistent, and it will happen. Thanks to you, the one who inspires and initiates.

▪ No Risk, No Innovation

In June 2014, the San Antonio Spurs won the NBA championship. The team's perennial star, Tim Duncan, has a career field goal percentage of .506, and for three-pointers it's .176.

Tim Duncan fails to make a basket 49.4 percent of the time. And when he hoists up a shot from three-point range, that rate of failure climbs to 82.4 percent.

Similarly, there is a success ratio when it comes to innovation. A company's appetite for failure during difficult times can shrivel, as the realization that innovation means "outcome uncertainty." Not every idea can, or will, be a winner.

Innovation—and the budgets to support it—become big, fat, juicy targets.

But champions of organizational innovation must have, and encourage, a *tolerance for failure* and *enthusiasm for risk taking*. For without risk, there can be no innovation. Fear of failure is anathema to innovation. Your team will be afraid to act, decide, move forward, and do the work it's capable of.

Food for thought: As this is written, a story is circulating about Alan Mulally, formerly of Boeing, who was brought in by William Ford to shake up the automobile maker. Mulally's style? High energy, laser focus, open to candid communication.

Not judgmental.

Long story short: Early in his tenure, he received a report that a line of new cars was delayed due to technical problems. His response? Mulally applauded the bearer of bad news. His message? Unlike certain competitors, where bad news was punished (and, therefore, hidden from top management until the point of international crisis), the signal was that at Ford, executives would be respected for being forthright about bad news. Let your people feel safe to fail, but empower them to do their best work. Failure should be seen and used as a learning experience.

▪ NPD Process—A Must!

In my opinion, a formalized NPD (new product development) process—frequently referred to as a Stage-Gate process*—is a must (although as you'll read later, some of my colleagues may disagree).

The process, in essence, has two key elements. The **stage** refers to the critical activities that need to be undertaken at a particular stage of product development.

The **gating** process involves ownership, decision makers, criteria, prioritization, and a degree of flexibility. This includes a selection of ideas and concepts from the hopper.

Overall, it is important to note that the NPD process must be a cross-business function. It requires balanced ownership between both the marketing and technology units. Therefore, all business functions must be aware of the process and engaged.

Communication of relevant information is essential, and key personnel should be involved in the go/no-go gating reviews. Productivity during product development can be achieved if, and only if, goals are clearly defined along the way and each process has contingencies clearly outlined on paper.

*Stage-Gate is a registered service mark of Stage-Gate International.

▪ Ownership

Most would agree that innovation is everyone's responsibility. However, innovation needs ownership, a champion within the organization. The champion must convince others to take calculated risks and work outside of one's own comfort zone. A successful leader is able to transform team members into stakeholders.

Often the most successful product development managers are the most facile, accomplished, and successful salespeople within the company. Why? Because, as the leader, sometimes you have to be able to build consensus around a new untested idea and have a disparate group of people rally for a cause with an uncertain outcome.

▪ Value

The fundamental purpose of innovation is to create value, which translates into money for customers and shareholders. All the processes, all the creativity, all the time, the effort, the research, the dreaming, the refining, the modeling, and the re-testing—what's it all for?

To enhance shareholder value. To build incremental revenues by filling a consumer need. And to polish your brand in the process. Sustainable process-driven innovation transforms ideas into vital intellectual property, intellectual property into revenues, and revenues into increased shareholder value.

Customer value can be created through the actual benefits of the new product, once you find that delicate balance between cost, price, and return. It is essential to get customer input and feedback during development in order to create—ideally—a launching customer.

As for shareholder value, this comes in two ways. First,

as return on investment (ROI). Enhanced product value be-gets higher margins and greater returns. Taking a longer-term viewpoint, a key driver of shareholder value is through patents. Patents protect and define the innovation and are the key step on the way to commercialization and enhancing value. It is imperative that—in the quest for enhanced value through in-novation—companies protect their technology and expertise through aggressive patenting programs.

Renew, refresh, and update regularly with new patents. Despite the expense, it is more than worthwhile. Patenting is a powerful value driver.

▪ Accountability: Innovation's Foundation

Action items that don't get done. Incentives that don't work. NPD programs that lose traction, despite the best, brightest, most passionate innovation owners. It's a frustrating thing when the process becomes akin to "herding cats." That is why one of the most important imperatives of **Robert's Rules of Innovation** is Accountability.

Accountability is a critical component of the trust equa-tion. From the outset, every member of the team has to com-mit to deadlines and be accountable to each other, to other departments, and to outside forces.

Team members need to feel responsibility for delivery. Slippage is the sure way to jeopardize the entire NPD process.

The innovation process owner must inculcate the group with the "one for all, all for one" mentality if your NPD pro-gram is to move to new heights.

(Note: Our survey of one hundred executives—see www. innovationcoach.com for details—found that a sense of ac-countability is one of the "most difficult" things to create with-in organizational culture of any kind.)

- ### Training (and Coaching)

Training is the often forgotten imperative to success in innovation, yet companies like Whirlpool believe it is, and have proven it to be, one of the most important imperatives to succeed in innovation. In many ways, innovation is all about the management of human resources. Finding, nurturing, and retaining the right people for the right slots can work magic for your NPD efforts.

Proper hiring, training, and coaching are the ways to creating, reinforcing, and enhancing company culture and mind-set. This attitude needs to come from the top and, in our most admired firms, it frequently represents the ethos of the founder.

We stressed this in our first book, and I feel so strongly about it that I am including it here as well: innovative companies are not necessarily created by establishing a separate and discrete Department of Innovation.

Rather, it's important for *the company* to be innovative, through and through. Strive to become the type of organization that attracts and rewards those who are open-minded and view it as a positive attribute, not a threat. Look for those with a natural curiosity, open-mindedness, and an ability to see the big picture—combined with hard-headed business acumen. Those with a left-brain/right-brain approach are pure gold, valuable to the success of the culture of innovation you seek to implement.

- ### Idea Management

Ideation, or idea management processes/system for LTD (long-term development), is essential to the NPD process. This is where the future's "wild ideas" come from, and it should be harnessed by a process with dedicated resources and with

NPD and LTD teams working together.

Bear in mind that the funnel needs to be filled to "feed" NPD, but champions need to also consider separate long-term development efforts. LTD has its own discrete R&D, testing and retesting, before concepts are winnowed down to viable NPD concepts that then make their way to the end of the funnel.

A brief note about negativity. Surely, you've heard it at ideation sessions:

"That will never work!"

"We tried that years ago; it was a disaster!"

"We don't have budget for *that*!"

At your ideation session, remember: there are no bad ideas. Of course, we know that there *are*! But the idea is to encourage participation, with all concepts written, filed, prioritized, and validated for future reference. Like sales items and raw goods, ideas should be inventoried. Stay open to new ideas, read blogs, and capture consumer insights—innovations can come from anywhere.

- **Observe (Measure and Track . . .)**

Observation, measurement, and tracking of NPD results are essential to optimal ROI. Create your baselines first, with initial observations and measurements. Then capture the time to each gate, the time spent inside each gate, etc.

Look for improvements in terms of reduction of time spent within each gate. Once a product is launched, a key metric is the ratio of NPD sales to overall sales. One method would be to track historical new product sales for the first three years after launch versus total sales. This is a baseline. Next, set a target goal for this ratio, based on your needs, and taking into consideration your competitive environment and the competition's baseline. This would be further calibrated to account for the product lifestyle in a particular industry, but in any case, new product sales are measured as a percentage of the total.

It's fascinating to watch when you are making headway. You see your margins growing as the right mix of new products comes onstream.

Product life cycles keep getting shorter, which mandates accelerated NPD cycles. In the personal care arena, for example, life cycles are only two to three years. So each big idea has tremendous potential value—it's important not to kill a potential success too early.

▪ Net Result . . . Reward

When it's all said and done, innovation is about ROI derived from the chemistry of ideas to money. Innovation: everyone wins. With profitable growth comes benefits to shareholders, stakeholders, employees, customers, and consumers—through market share gain, new products, and new features.

Accelerating the process is the promise of equitable financial reward for those who drive the NPD process to new heights. In my experience, many have benefited from remuneration packages that reward the head of R&D via a percentage of sales from new products.

Remember, too, that incentives are needed for all participants, and that includes your development staff. Frequently, the key motivator is less financial and more for recognition for a job well-done, validation for their Zen-like ability to conjure new concepts and test and retest prototypes. So just FYI— motivation isn't always about money, but motivation is critical.

Look for *Robert's Rules of Innovation* at your favorite bookseller to get much more depth and insight around these imperatives. It is truly the foundation for any structured repeatable process and success in innovation.

Why "The Art of Implementation"?

The short answer is because—as a consultant to companies large and small around the world—I see, over and over, all the best intentions, all the hard work and energy toward creation of an innovation culture, go down the drain. The predominant reason? The inability of the organization to implement the innovation plans management has agreed upon. While most organizations believe that innovation is required to remain competitive in today's marketplace, they often do not put enough emphasis on building the organizational capability for innovation.

At this point in my career, I've seen enough to understand the power of innovation, and the organization-wide— even industry-wide—fear it can create. Innovation means disruption of the status quo, and this disruption is not without consequences. And while some may argue that disruptive innovation is a competitive strategy for an "age seized by terror," I would say disruptive innovation is an argument against complacency, made more relevant by a landscape transformed by technology. Take, for example, the recent changes that have occurred in the recorded music industry.

Not since recordings supplanted the sale of sheet music has the music industry seen such a tumultuous upheaval. Barriers are being broken, largely by—and for—the millennial generation.

Think about it: no longer are "record sales" (already a quaint expression) enough to help a musician or band succeed. The model of creating pieces of plastic, placing them in stores, and generating revenue via sales is dead. The metric of "sales" is about to sink completely, without a trace.

The biggest record album of all time is Michael Jackson's *Thriller*, with more than $100 million in sales. In comparison, a pop singer such as Pitbull, with fifty million Facebook fans and 170 million plays on YouTube, has yet to sell ten million albums.

Today the industry is all about the sale of concert tickets and ancillary products. Brand owners spend big on community building by sponsoring venues, festivals, concerts, and more.

In the meantime, digital streaming services such as Spotify, Pandora, Deezer, SoundCloud, and Napster Unlimited deliver tunes to users via their ubiquitous mobile devices. But buying the artist's music? Nah. Not with millennials. Millennials have grown up in a world full of choices. They are buying—they're just buying differently.

As a result, the $240 million earned last year by the top ten music acts represents less than 20 percent of the billion dollars brands will spend to build customer relationships with digital natives.

In terms of music creation, artists can now create recordings without ever setting foot in a studio. Today, it's all about the digital audio workstation (DAW). Apple's Logic Pro X is a nifty one. The MSRP? $199.99. For $200, why bother with pesky union musicians or practice music scales? With the inexpensive, professional-quality DAW, the artist easily navigates the entire recording process, including virtual instruments, editing, and more. Need a tutorial on various features? Search YouTube and you'll find no shortage of how-tos.

The millennial generation can now easily create, distribute, and share music. The middleman has a diminished role.

Sounds great. And it *is* great, since the new model allows efficient pairing of music makers and music consumers. But where does that leave commercial radio, or classical music? Or people who play "actual" instruments? Or music producers, sound engineers, studio people? Where does that leave label employees? Come to think of it, where does it leave anyone who ever had a financial stake in the playing, recording, distribution, and sales of recorded music?

So, yes, the fear of innovation is understandable. And yet, implementation of innovation is a must if we, as a world community, are to advance.

At this point, it might be instructive to visit Amsterdam back in the year 1585. I was born and raised in The Netherlands, and I hope this trip in my Dutch-made time machine resonates as much for you as it does for me.

Back in the late sixteenth century, Amsterdam benefitted from a great influx of newcomers, largely from Antwerp, a city that fell to Spanish soldiers that year. Antwerp was the business and cultural capital of northern Europe at the time, and those who left for Amsterdam were, generally speaking, successful members of the merchant class.

In addition to their financial resources, they arrived in Amsterdam steeped in the culture of economic innovation, as espoused by Austrian economist Joseph Schumpeter. His premise was that "creative destruction" was a driver of capitalism and that relentless innovation kept the economy on the boil—with the new "creatively" destroying the old.

According to Schumpeter—and this is reported brilliantly in *Amsterdam: A History of the World's Most Liberal City* by Rus-

http://commons.wikimedia.org (no permission required)
Artist: Jacob Knyff

sell Shorto—the spark that ignites the economic innovation that keeps an economy healthy and growing is attributable to a tiny group of people.

And, he states, this small group of innovators is almost never part of the status quo, or establishment. Rather, a small group of newbies spot opportunities and drive change, in the face of risks and obstacles, and—in time—succeed. This group is followed by succeeding waves of newcomer-innovators, pushing the previous generation's "breakthroughs" into the mainstream.

Shorto points out a key differentiator within Amsterdam. Specifically, the city did not inhibit anyone from doing business there in the late sixteenth century. The freedom of new immigrants to participate in the economic process helped the area become a hotbed of economic success.

Those people, hundreds of years ago, understood that we must implement innovation if we are to thrive. Yes, innovation is difficult and can result in traumatic economic dislocations for those on the wrong side of history.

Therefore, I always remind my colleagues of the importance of "continuous improvement." And for those who shy away from innovation out of fear, I repeat this: "failure" is a learning experience.

A key to successful, long-term innovation implementation is the willingness and effort to break down this daunting goal into small, digestible steps. For example, I advise leaders to set corporate and/or group goals and create a motto that communicates this common purpose. At one company I led, Airspray International, we boldly stated: "One Innovation per Year"— and we doggedly stuck to it.

Another important tactic is making the implementation of innovation personal by appointing a departmental champion, entrusted with getting the job done. To make this happen, we create a structured, repeatable process, such as Stage-Gate, and hold monthly management meetings, where the best of the best innovations are ranked and re-ranked—because innovation portfolio management is critical to successful implementation.

At the top of the list is the need to get everybody involved and make sure that the workplace environment is—and will continue to be—conducive to the collaboration it takes to get the job done. This requires proper alignment of objectives and rewards.

Let me stress this: proper innovation implementation is wholly dependent upon collaboration. It should not be thought of as something that is inflicted upon people but, rather, something that is done *with* people.

Begin the process with sensitivity and the knowledge that change management is tricky and yet an imperative. Let your team understand the big picture—goals, hopes, and aspirations—as opposed to a negatively charged environment that focuses upon what does not currently exist. In so doing, we permit the key stakeholders to fully comprehend how things will work once the program is fully implemented. As for the actual process, however, it is critical to provide the flexibility to permit midcourse corrections rather than maintaining an adherence to a policy that stymies smooth, long-term implementation. You know what? It's impossible to predict the future, so why plan it in microscopic detail?

The challenges and barriers to innovation implementation, you see, are daunting, and the reason is because they are largely related to human resources. They are people issues, and they require patience (and intestinal fortitude) as well as structure.

In his great book *What Would Google Do?*, author Jeff Jarvis notes that Google gives its technical employees "a license to pursue your dreams," as the company's Marissa Mayer first termed this approach in *Fast Company* magazine. That is, these employees have the chance—strike that, they are *required*—to use 20 percent of their time to work on new products, ventures, and ideas. It's a requirement, part of the job. Mayer was quoted as saying that half the new products and features launched by the company in one six-month period came from work completed under the 20 percent rule.

You, as your organization's innovator-in-chief, must find a way to creatively manage the people and processes needed to successfully implement your process. Your people must be fully involved and your project's success must be carefully defined within the business strategy of your organization.

Furthermore, your commitment to properly implementing innovation must come at the right moment.

Why Now?

There are a variety of tipping points throughout the history of an organization that will cause the leader to fully comprehend the need for innovation implementation.

It may be a long drought of revenue growth.

Perhaps you've lost a succession of big new business pitches.

One or more big accounts just left for a competitor.

Your industry is raving about a new product, service, or concept that just hit the market—and, once again, it's not yours.

Whatever the tipping point, whatever the aha moment, when it comes you have to act! Innovation is not a luxury. It's a must-have. Especially these days, with a flood of new products and flankers hitting store shelves.

Sometimes, the tipping point seems to come unexpectedly, although in their heart of hearts, insiders knew that the "sudden cataclysmic event" was all but inevitable.

With the luxury of twenty-twenty hindsight, we could have all predicted the "Kodak moment"—that is, when the venerable company filed Chapter 11. As I mentioned earlier with the music industry reference, process technology is under tremendous pressure (niche market sales of vinyl recordings and turntables notwithstanding).

My friend and fellow agent for innovation Paul Hobcraft puts it well in his penetrating Paul4Innovating's blog. Paul correctly observes that similar transitions (a polite way to put it!) are impacting newspapers, book publishers, movie studios, broadcasting, and more. "It is new technology that is reaping the destruction," he wrote. While he admits that digital images "are certainly easier to store," he bemoans the lack of emotional connection: "no feel, no tactile effect."

However, his issue—and the salient point here—is that "Kodak was well aware of the future." They failed to face it head-on with a strategy that needed to be more transformational, revolutionary, or evolutionary. Today, he correctly concludes of Kodak, which, as we know, invented digital photography and yet failed to convert the technology to a viable proposition moving forward, "companies simply disappear if they don't do great things, executed well and on-time, to stop destruction hammering at their door . . ."

What Does Innovation Mean to *You*? Your *Company*?

Some companies are content to take an innovation breather—resting upon past successes or making incremental changes to successful products. Others are looking at ways to reposition existing technologies in order to appeal to new end-user audiences.

Before we head further into our innovation implementation journey, it would be wise for us to define terms. What do we mean by *innovation*?

A common misconception I see in the business world is the confusion between "innovation" and "strategy." Innovation, in and of itself, is certainly not a strategy. Innovation, to my mind, is the WD-40 of an organization. It is used to free up corporate strategies such as profitable growth, product/service differentiation, or new product development.

Innovation, when properly applied—like WD-40 metaphor—can help achieve these strategic goals. "Innovation for the sake of 'innovation'" is a distortion—a misuse of a very powerful and beneficial tool.

As the innovation program is implemented, it is extremely important to make sure the output is aligned with organizational goals. Failure to ensure this alignment may sway internal opinion away from further innovative activity and can result in the opposite of the desired effect.

Think of it this way: strategy and innovation are both different—and both essential. Strategy provides the direction, the form. It is not simply "well thought out"—a value. Rather, it is a framework within which decisions can be made that help the organization progress. Proper strategy is crystalline, elegant. It is understandable and clear. It is not confused corporate-speak.

It—strategy—exists solely to serve the success of the organization.

Technological cycles are shorter and shorter these days and can also impact business models (see also: Kodak, as noted previously). Thus, innovation's ability to modify strategy is critical. This explains why innovation implementation—an ongoing, successful innovation program—must exist separately and distinctly from overall corporate strategy.

"New and improved." To some, this phrase encapsulates their understanding of "innovation." In fact, innovation is overused and misapplied. Let's take a moment to clarify and distinguish between the three general forms of innovation:

Breakthrough innovation can disrupt an industry. In the realm of personal care products, such an innovation might include a product or ingredient that delivers an all-new market application—in the form of a breakthrough finished product.

Continuous innovation refers to a new product that requires no, or little, change in consumer behavior. Example: the latest version of your favorite smartphone.

Dynamically continuous innovation refers to a significant adjustment in consumer behavior. Example: moving from liquid hand soaps to the one-touch, mechanical foamers pioneered at my former company, Airspray International.

In each case, however, it is important to note that the key is not a technology or ingredient, but understanding how the consumer (or end user) must alter behavior/usage. The key to successful innovation, therefore, rests upon identifying—and solving—a specific end-user need, rather than developing a technology, per se.

There are three ways to look at innovation, and all of them address the ultimate goal: creating value in the minds of your customers, whether you sell B2B or directly to end users/consumers.

Having said all that, what are the key concerns regarding getting started?

Another way to look at this is: where do you place your bets when it comes to understanding end-user needs and investing in innovation?

For this, I asked my Amsterdam-based colleague Costas Papaikonomou, cofounder of Happen Group, the innovation agency. He notes, first, that there is a dynamic tension between technical and marketing teams, in terms of looking to future needs and setting timelines.

"Ask your R&D team how long it takes to develop a particular capability, and the default answer is five years," he says. "Ask marketing what new products they expect to need in five years, and they'll tell you what they need next year."

"In essence, both teams are right," Papaikonomou argues. If you read between the lines, both teams are really saying: "We don't know how the future will affect us."

According to Papaikonomou, there are four steps in analyzing the question, before answering it:

Explore future scenarios first. Go further out than you'd ever be comfortable with for ROI calculations. It's OK. Have your technical and commercial teams spend some quality time together on thinking up what the world will look like in five to ten years' time, how the changes will affect your industry, your category, your markets. Ideate for fifteen to twenty product or service concepts that would do well in your future world. This is the easy part, because everything is obvious in foresight.

Chart and rank what technical capabilities you'd need to create them. For every one of your future concepts, list up to three new capabilities you would need to have matured in order to deliver them profitably. Go "360" here: review technology, supply chain, sourcing, distribution, etcetera. Now chart the overlap. Which capabilities appear over and over, as critical for multiple concepts? You're getting warmer now; most likely a top five of core capabilities is emerging, the platforms that will give you most bang for buck wherever the future winners turn out to be.

Review their implications, and then some more. This is where it gets fun. For each of the key capabilities, list the implications across your business (internal) and market (external) of implementing them. Then list the implications of those implications. You'll be surprised at what that second round reveals. Most likely, your list of core capabilities halved along the way, and at least one new joiner appeared.

Play to win or play to be in the game? Make or buy? The last step is surprisingly easy and shamefully often overlooked. "Make or buy?" Practice saying that out loud in front of a mirror, and then in front of your technical team; it will turn heads. For some reason, too many people think everything needs to be developed from scratch. Look again at your short list of capabilities you need in order to thrive in the future, in the context of what passed in all three steps before. Which of them are actually mere nice-to-haves, platform standards that most likely already exist in other industries? Just *buy* them, now. What are the ownable, differentiating capabilities you want to excel at and win? *Make* them or buy the companies that make them. Start developing and patenting like there's no tomorrow.

"Charting innovation bets and deciding where to invest your R&D money becomes much easier once you realize you don't need twenty-twenty vision on what the future will bring, nor spreading the bet across a huge number of alternatives," he says. "As long as you know what you need to be good at—that's critical."

As for open innovation, which is an effective method for gaining ideas from outside an organization, it is important to remember that to achieve long-term, sustained innovation, companies need to establish a structured, repeatable process. Breakthrough innovations still have to come from within the company through hard work and consistent efforts.

Not all innovations have to be of the breakthrough variety. Line extensions and next-generation products keep the momentum going as well.

And last, remember that while there is supreme pressure to innovate, and despite our best intentions, innovation can still find itself taking a backseat to the rigors of the day-to-day. You will always need to close deals, pacify customers, and hit your numbers. Plus, innovation can be frightening because we are only human, and we can be afraid of change and, even worse, terrified of failure.

Especially in an uncertain job market.

In spite of it all, you must ask yourself: What have I done to facilitate implementation of innovation? Have I helped create an environment that rewards controlled risk and allows for the failure that inevitably comes with innovation implementation?

THINK ABOUT:

- Know your consumer demand drivers, inside and out.
- Make sure your corporate ecosystem is saturated with consumer knowledge.
- Innovate to support corporate strategy/goals, not to emulate your competitor's list of attributes.
- Take your end user's position and be fearlessly disruptive on that consumer's behalf.

CHAPTER

Innovation Assassination

> Our wretched species is so made that those who
> walk on the well-trodden path always throw
> stones at those who are showing a new road.
> —Voltaire, *Philosophical Dictionary*

"We tried that once already!"
"We don't have budget for that!"
"Our clients will never go for it!"

Sound familiar? These are just a few of the typical comments from those who, for a variety of reasons, prefer innovation assassination to innovation implementation.

Why does it happen? How can you win over the chronic naysayers and effectively implement a sustainable culture of innovation in your workplace?

Let's first break the issue into its key components and examine them.

Why Does It Happen?

Sometimes innovation assassination thrives in larger organizations. The bigger the outfit, the more difficult it is for innovation to flow. In such cases, it becomes essential to break down silos and territorial divisions and open up channels of communication. For lurking in the deep, dark recesses of your organization are the assassins, lying in wait, ready to snipe and oh-so-eager to keep their death grip on their beloved status quo.

The power of the status quo over hearts and minds never ceases to amaze me. I frequently listen to top executives insist—quite earnestly and with a completely straight face—how much they want to change the culture of their organization, encourage fresh thinking, and break up the bonds of the status quo.

But as the conversation continues, it becomes readily apparent that these self-professed "agents for change" cling to the status quo as tightly as a drowning man holds on to a life raft.

Sometimes, it is pure fear. Fear of failure. Fear of the unknown. Fear of criticism. Fear of change. Fear of being terminated. In today's business climate, one might have compassion for those who harbor such fears. For, in reality, so many of the folks I consult with, in a wide variety of industries, feel as if they are on the bubble. That is, one false move and—poof!—they're on the street.

The residual effects of the Great Recession still reverberate down the hallways of today's public- and private-sector organizations. When your team feels insecure, whether that insecurity is justified or not, it is more prone to innovation assassination. In the great chess game of life, they are in self-preservation mode—bunker mentality, playing defense, and, worse, playing "not to lose" rather than to win the game. It's human nature and, to a degree, it's understandable. They are removing what they perceive to be a mortal threat: change.

In some organizations, however, the root cause of innovation assassination is purely political. This can be ugly. We've all witnessed the death-by-torpedo of exciting new thinking, because of the "not invented here" syndrome ("no one will get credit for cool stuff around me unless it is me, and my group"). Sometimes, the political motivation is nothing more complicated than the battle between warring factions jockeying over organizational turf.

And then there are cases where innovation assassination is a direct result of an organization's decades of DNA, ingrained cultural cues. Dogma, if you will. Resistance to "the other" will be fierce and often have very little to do with the actual worth or validity of the innovation being proposed. Call it inertia, call it closed-mindedness, call it ridiculous, call it whatever you wish.

When It's Time to Hatch the Egg

Another fairly common innovation assassination behavior I see in my consulting work is what I refer to as "analysis paralysis." Personally, I tend to take an action-oriented approach. Analysis, reason, care, and intelligence—of course—must be part of the equation. However, there comes a point in time when some leaders have a tough time hatching the egg, so to speak. They insist on revisiting what has already been determined, over and over and over again. It becomes a deadly bias against action, an attempt to seek perfection, at the expense of missing the boat.

Of course, there are industries where innovation implementation is tied tightly to regulation, such as the healthcare profession. However, would you agree that in many other instances, there comes a time when "too much research"— or the need to reach "perfection"—is actually causing you to miss serious market opportunities?

Here's an example that was widely reported in 2013, involving a favorite movie maker, Pixar. Apropos of "analysis paralysis," you'll be interested to learn that even with eleven hit movies, Pixar cofounder and president Ed Catmull describes Pixar's creative process as "going from suck to nonsuck."

That is a direct quote.

In fact, it would seem that Catmull and Pixar's directors find it preferable to fine-tune problems than to avoid mistakes. "My strategy has always been: be wrong as fast as we can," says Andrew Stanton, director of *Finding Nemo* and *WALL-E*. Or, *as I wrote in the original Robert's Rules of Innovation, "fail fast and fail cheap."* Stanton summarizes, "We're gonna screw up, let's just admit that. Let's not be afraid of that."

Believe it or not, Pixar starts each new movie idea with rough storyboards. No script. *No script!* Storyboards are then painstakingly refined until problems are resolved and the movie eventually evolves from "suck to nonsuck," as the studio head so colorfully puts it.

"Every time we show a film for the first time, it sucks," Catmull has said. Those within the organization and test audiences send their comments to the director (à la crowdsourcing) and explain likes and dislikes.

Supposedly, a favorite of mine, *Finding Nemo*, had a narrative continuity issue regarding some flashbacks that test audiences didn't understand. *Toy Story 2* required a complete stem-to-stern rewrite just months before its theatrical release. The good news is that Pixar film release dates are firm. These irreversible deadlines prevent Pixar from getting lost in the pursuit of perfection.

The point is, Pixar cultivates ideation, not immediate perfection.

Please don't get me wrong. Striving for perfection, maintaining the highest of standards, planning for the future, and implementing an innovation process is not wrong. Far from it. And perfectionism does not categorically block creativity.

However, I have seen organizations cower from innovation implementation, under the guise of "striving for perfection." That, I believe, is where the process becomes counterproductive.

The baseball slugger in a profound slump can tend to over-think his or her approach at the plate, watch too much film, or ruminate over the advice of the hitting coach. In this state, the hitter is afraid of striking out again, of making a mistake and letting the team down.

Other players understand the nature of their profession. They put in their work in the batting cage, sure, but ultimately they trust their talent. By extension, Pixar's culture is defined by a pursuit of excellence and quality. It is allowable to go from suck to nonsuck while in the development process. It is an environment where steady, relentless refinement is encouraged and rewarded, a company that promotes ongoing prototyping and experimentation.

What impresses me most is the lack of cultural self-consciousness around failure. The boss readily admits it: the first iteration is going to suck. They don't care! But the entire team understands that by remaining less emotionally invested in initial failure, they are freer to put the early failures behind them and work, together, toward the common goal: another fabulous hit, another milestone in cinematic entertainment.

Dealing with innovation assassination, then, becomes a matter of recognizing the various root causes of this pathology and taking proactive steps toward creation of a culture where the freedom to fail flourishes.

A big part of this is the role of the leader in delivering praise and deflecting criticism. Most of you, I'm sure, would agree on this: "When success comes in, the leader should give the credit to the team members. When failure comes, the leader should absorb the criticism and protect the team members."

The reality, however, is that while management is routinely bombarded with innovation management tips, typically they emphasize that creation of a risk-taking environment is essential—but do not specify how.

Even among managers, there is broad consensus that the risk of failure must be accepted by the organization, coupled with cynicism and a pervasive opinion that such intents and statements simply do not work. In far too many instances, rewards go to those who adopt the typical, safe, and trusted methods and deliver fault-free work.

Fight the Culture of Fear

So what practical steps can organizations take to promote risk taking among their employees? Are there different kinds of failures or errors?

The key, I believe, is to encourage the "creative error." Further, organizations cannot afford to ignore *all* errors with the aim of encouraging creative errors.

At one end of the spectrum, there are errors arising due to sabotage or intentional concealment of errors made or noticed by employees. Leadership reaction to these has to be zero tolerance and strong disapproval. Otherwise it will confound employees. A perfect example of this, as I write this in 2014, is the sad situation involving treatment wait times at the US Department of Veterans' Affairs' health-care facilities.

In the middle of the spectrum, there are errors due to carelessness, unwillingness to learn, inadequate capabilities, and other such reasons. Some organizations can build up an unhealthy tolerance for these, even as they do not actively sanction them.

And then, at the other end of the spectrum, are *creative errors*. These occur due to changing market circumstances, calculated risks and rewards, and bad timing. Innovators please note: these are the ones to spot and encourage in your organization.

There is, then, a right and wrong type of failure. I propose a selective approach that can help to encourage the right errors and foster the elusive spirit of risk taking that all organizations strive for.

A perfect example is the Tata Group Innovation Forum (yes, I know: TGIF). Tata is most widely known for its tradition of innovation in a variety of industries. Most notably, the company's brand portfolio now includes such iconic automotive marques as Jaguar and Land Rover.

Some years ago, the company added a new award, called Dare to Try, in its group-wide Tata Innovation program. Under this program, company managers and teams are encouraged to send in entries for innovations that were attempted, but which failed to get to the marketplace for one reason or another. Entries are reviewed by peer managers in ten regional rounds. Finalists are reviewed by an external jury in Mumbai.

The program visibility throughout the company is high. Winners are honored by the company's chairman at a widely broadcast corporate function.

One year, the winner of the Dare to Try award was the TMETC (Tata Motors Engineering Technical Centre, UK), which failed to develop an innovative IVT (infinitely variable transmission) for the company's ultra-compact Nano car. Within the tight timelines, TMETC could not deliver a target cost and performance-effective product. "The team does not consider their IVT endeavor a failure. TMETC and Tata Motors fought a good fight—and won more than it lost," reported the internal publication.

Another operating unit, Tata Technologies, had acquired a company called INCAT Inc. and began development of software for instructor-led distance learning. The team's achievements were noteworthy. Students could learn on their own computers with flexible times, at their convenience. Lessons could be repeated and one-to-one and live instructor assistance was made available. However, there were a number of user-interface issues and the program failed to launch. Unlike firms that would treat such failures harshly, within Tata the program was praised as another honoree in its Dare to Try program.

Companies such as these understand an intrinsic aspect of innovation implementation, one that helps breed a culture of fear. Specifically, I'm talking about the inherent conflict between innovation and operations.

The Battle: Innovation vs. Operations

The very purpose of innovation is to change things up, to move processes forward, and to disrupt the status quo.

Operations, on the other hand, thrive when every activity and process is repeatable, predictable, and smooth. Under such conditions, standards can be set and efficiencies of time and labor can be optimized.

What, then, is the very antithesis of repeatability and predictability? Exactly—innovation. Innovation, by definition, walks the tightrope of uncertainty. And it's not as if one side of the equation is "wrong" and the other side is "right." The lesson here is that innovation and operations have two very different points of origin. Where innovation is about looking to the midterm or long-term benefit, operations are all about short-term goals. If it is new, if it is uncertain, if it can fail, it has no place being bundled in, or near, operations.

Savvy leaders understand this dichotomy and make every effort to defuse those who would be innovation assassins—and help them accept (or at the very least, deal with) their aversion to innovation. Innovation assassins often work under the pretense of being constructive, yet they actively look to find flaws in anything new and untested. It can be hard to mitigate these would-be assassins, but the best approach is by reinforcing a culture that accepts, and even encourages, disruption.

And it seems to be working. As I write this, global powerhouse GE has just unveiled the results of its 2014 Global Innovation Barometer. The GE Global Innovation Barometer conducts annual surveys to put a finger on the pulse of innovation around the world. The survey was conducted earlier this year with more than 3,200 high-level business executives from more than twenty-six participating countries and examines the transformative actions that senior business executives take to pursue innovation.

In contrast to previous years, the report (which is available at www.ideaslaboratory.com) indicates that most thought leaders and executives embrace disruption and actively call for transformation within their organizations. The barometer points out that while many have yet to find the perfect business model, "most are embracing the adaptation to new innovation trends— as well as searching for the new kinds of talent, technology, and partners they need to become disruption ready." Leaders have taken control of their "innovation vertigo" and are finding balance by developing a tolerance for failure, an enthusiasm for risk taking, and a willingness to invest without ROI assurance.

Even in the face of shifting behaviors, problems still exist. There is no clear "go-to-market" strategy. Respondents seem equally split between the desire to race to market and the desire to perfect their product before reaching consumers. In addition, businesses will need to pay extra attention when recruiting top talent. While 79 percent of executives say that "talent is critical for innovation success," only 32 percent believe that their organization excels at attracting and retaining it.

According to Beth Comstock, senior vice president and chief marketing officer of GE, "Change is everywhere, and this year's Barometer shows how, more than ever, leaders are embracing the new models and technologies critical to innovating today and making their businesses 'disruption ready.' Innovation at GE is about developing new markets and technologies to drive growth. We are partnering and learning from start-ups and entrepreneurs, finding ways to be a faster and simpler company, and using big data." Disrupt or be disrupted.

Without a way to combat the innovation assassins, imagine how difficult it would have been for Milwaukee's Harley-Davidson to introduce its Project LiveWire electric motorcycle.

Harley-Davidson LiveWire electric motorcycle
Source: iStock Images

It's fast, it's smooth—and it's virtually silent. No rumble from the iconic V-Twin engine configuration that stirs the hearts of legions of fans around the world. The initial version of this bike has an estimated range of a mere fifty-three miles. No room for saddlebags. Not even a passenger seat. These factors would seem to be anathema to the brand's core constituency. Yet Harley-Davidson representatives are, as this is written, trucking their new bikes to major dealers and motorcycle gatherings around the world, offering test rides.

They ask only one thing in return: opinions. This input will be tossed into the stew and the stealthily quiet Project Live-Wire will be taken right back to the drawing board, if their core followers demand it.

But imagine, for a second, the guts it took for the iconic brand built on the rumble of a V-Twin to turn its focus to electric.

From the Mind of Google

It is instructive at this point to examine how Google approaches the problem of innovation assassination. In fact, the company recently updated its Nine Principles of Innovation. These are the underlying tenets of the company's innovation drivers, designed as a corporate "line in the sand" for any possible doubters. I suggest we all think about them, in the context of our own companies.

1. Innovation comes from anywhere.

This principle, which also made former executive Marissa Mayer's 2008 list, points out that innovation is in nobody's job title at Google but is everyone's responsibility. (Mayer, as this is written, is fighting hard for the future of Yahoo!, as that company's president and CEO.)

Ideas come from anyone—from the very top of the organization on down.

Google Glass, for example, was actively promoted by the company's cofounder, Sergey Brin. Google Health product manager Dr. Roni Zeiger was the one who suggested that the company should optimize information on suicide prevention hotlines whenever a related search is conducted.

2. Focus on the user.

This, again, is a long-standing Google principle. The company encourages employees to build products with the user—not profits—in mind, and "revenue issues take care of themselves," said Gopi Kallayil, chief evangelist at Google for Brand Marketing, at a recent conference.

3. Think 10x, not 10 percent.

This is a new one, driven by Google cofounder Larry Page's preference for radical innovation over incremental improvements.

The principle of making a tenfold difference is what drove projects such as Project Loon, where Google uses high-altitude balloons to bring Wi-Fi connections to remote areas.

4. Bet on technical insights.

Number four is an update of the company's previous principle: "Data is apolitical."

Google's self-driving cars are an example of how Google strives to tie its various information assets together to create all-new product entries.

"It all started with reading in the *Economist* that more than a million traffic deaths are caused a year by human error. The 10x thinking was if you removed humans from the picture then cars would be much safer.

"We had the building blocks to make that possible," he said, in reference to Google Maps and artificial intelligence technology based upon technology developed for its Street View cars.

5. Ship and iterate.

This is the latest version of Mayer's principle of "Innovation, not instant perfection"—and it directly ties back to a point I made earlier in this chapter about analysis paralysis.

Think about the company's launch of Google Glass. The company relies upon end-user feedback to finesse product development. Remember: Gmail was in beta for three years.

6. Twenty percent time.

The 20 percent rule, referenced earlier in this book, means Google requires ("encourages") employees to spend fully one-fifth of their time pursuing ideas they are passionate about.

Results of this program? How about Google News, Google Alerts, and off-road Google Maps Street View.

Corporate folklore has it that Google mechanical engineer Dan Ratner was frustrated when he couldn't map his route to a hotel in Spain. The roads were too narrow for Google's Street View cars to navigate. Google now mounts Street View cameras on bikes, trikes, and backpacks, to help widen the scope of coverage.

7. Default to open.

Melissa Mayer's original goal was to share information on Google's intranet and facilitate collaboration. Now, the company has furthered its foray into pulling ideas from the public.

"There are seven billion people. . . .The smartest people will always be outside Google," Kallayil said. "By defaulting to open, we're tapping into the creativity outside of Google."

The Android operating system is one example he gives—the OS claims 1.4 million new activations a day and a growing galaxy of applications and developers.

8. Fail well.

I like to say "fail fast and fail cheap." Google's phrase is "fail well." Either way, the point is that there should be *no negativity attached to failure.*

Think about the failed Google products, such as Buzz, Gears, Panoramio, and Wave. Google's take on it? According to Kallayil, failure is a "badge of honor."

"There is no stigma against failing," he said. "There is a belief in the company that if you don't fail often enough, you're not trying hard enough.

"Once we realize a product is not working out, we kill it, but the thing with products is they morph—we take all the best ideas and redeploy them."

Industry observers note that Google's social networking platform, Google Plus, incorporates elements of Google Buzz, Wave, Orkut, and OpenSocial.

9. Have a mission that matters.

This is a new principle for the company and "the most important one," Kallayil says. "Everybody at Google has a very strong sense of mission and purpose. We seriously believe that the work that we do has a huge impact on millions of people in a positive way."

Example: Google's Person Finder was up shortly after the earthquake and tsunami in Japan in early 2011, facilitating the search for victims and families.

Once again, I'll turn to my fellow innovator Paul Hobcraft to help frame the issue. We agree that organizational culture has an outsized influence on company direction. It influences strategy, management practice, behaviors, and performance. "Culture eats strategy for breakfast," he said.

Tackling the implementation of innovation means holding the reins of the people within your organization. Success depends upon leadership, not "disruption" or "removing constraints" or other buzzwords of the day.

Believe it or not, the University of Southern California (USC) has created a new academy "to inspire innovative, entrepreneurial thought in business, design, marketing, and the arts."

"The degree is in disruption," the school's website proudly proclaims. "Conceived as a collaborative environment that brings multidisciplinary students, instructors, and professional mentors together, the USC Jimmy Iovine and Andre Young Academy for Arts, Technology and the Business of Innovation will be a transformational presence on one of the nation's most dynamic university campuses."The focus is on invention and conceptual thinking, drawing on the talents and influences of leaders from across industries to empower the next generation of disruptive inventors and professional thought leaders across a multitude of global industries."

Jimmy Iovine is a record industry titan, producer extraordinaire, and past judge on *American Idol*. Andre (Dr. Dre) Young is a well-known rapper and producer who, along with Iovine, is the cofounder of Beats Electronics. Yes, the very Beats Electronics that (via Beats by Dre) has captured *40 percent* of the billion-dollar headphones industry. The company was just sold to Apple, packaged with streaming music service Beats Music, for a cool $3 billion. The pair donated $70 million to the school, which now has a Dr. Dre–branded program.

To me and many of my fellow innovators, however, such emphasis on "disruption" has executives looking through the wrong end of the telescope. True, change is disruptive, by definition. But what percentage of innovations can truly be termed "disruptive"? Is this kind of branding of higher education programs misleading to would-be business leaders and entrepreneurs of the future?

Must every innovation be "breakthrough" and, second, what is the place of constraint in the innovation process? There are those who would argue that constraints on thinking should be encouraged, as it pushes us to workable, real-world insights. Google's Marissa Mayer, when she was vice president of Search Product & User Experience, has been quoted as saying it helps to have some constraint to see a lot of innovation. "Constraints shape and focus problems, and provide clear challenges to overcome as well as inspiration. Creativity loves constraints, but they must be balanced with a healthy disregard for the impossible," said Mayer.

The idea that boundaries and limits can actually unshackle the inhibitions to our thinking seems counterintuitive. But in reality, many fields of creative endeavor are based upon limits, or rules, that shape the art form.

Now, in the beauty and personal care business, for example, the best players solve a consumer problem, or hit a key end-user "hot button" in a way that has never been seen before. The quest for "new" is a big driver. However, creation of such solutions requires extensive understanding of consumer needs, aspirations, and actual usage patterns. My former associate Jill McCurdy spent hours and hours with her team, talking to consumers about their cosmetics and actually watching how they used products in the context of their normal routine. Disruption, for the sake of pure . . . well, "disruption" may not actually prove successful in the crucible of the marketplace.

Amazon.com folklore has it that innovators write the press release *first*, before an idea is pitched to Jeff Bezos. The very process of organizing that short, fact-packed document helps snap the concept into laser focus.

Rather than pitching "disruption" and overusing a management term du jour, think about this: the climate for innovation can only thrive when every aspect of the organization promotes the creativity, engagement, and acceptance of the change that is required. This climate must be reinforced in governance, function, metrics, rewards, and more. It must be a 360-degree environment, baked into the cake. Trust must be earned. Once it is, the stage is set for increased commitment to a culture of innovation, where failure does not mean dismissal. This is the type of environment that encourages "free-range thinking" of the sort that leads to big moments.

And not just the "Eureka!" that occurs in a big meeting. I mean the sort of collegial, free-flowing ideation that happens over an after-work beer, at lunch, or whenever your people are loose, excited, and full of bonhomie.

What this optimal scenario tells us is that we, as innovation leaders and foes of the assassins, must take care to nurture the social synapses, or connections, that free your folks to talk across silos.

This trust building will help your teams with the confidence it takes to excel, and work hard, with great diligence, toward a common goal. And such trust can only come when leadership creates the processes that reward contributors and open the doors to participation.

Once objectives and reward systems are in alignment, conflicts are mitigated and output is optimized. Such a scenario makes it impossible for assassins to work their counterproductive black arts with impunity. For if your innovation drive is perceived as this month's fad, or management's latest bee in the bonnet, then it is doomed to fail and the naysayers will win. Again.

Paul Hobcraft has a great metaphor for these naysayers. He calls them organizational antibodies and correctly notes that they will fight the forces of innovation when they feel threatened.

Middle management has been especially vulnerable to corporate reorganizations since 2008 and, not surprisingly, this at-risk group—feeling especially threatened or misaligned— frequently goes all out blocking change and disrupting your innovation implementation. This insecure level favors the safe road and works feverishly to derail anything perceived as risky.

The bottom line is that you must recognize such pathologies and deal with them head-on, and for the long term. It is a difficult assignment, because there is so much at stake, both for you and your organization, and for those who fear change and, by extension, innovation. You and your company have to survive a tsunami of competitive threats. The naysayers, the innovation assassins, are in mortal fear for their jobs and their ability to pay their mortgages, get their kids educated, or save something for retirement.

Frankly, changing corporate culture can seem as daunting as making a U-turn in the Hudson River with the *Queen Mary II*.

But ultimately the success of your innovation implementation efforts depend upon your ability to—if necessary—do a gut renovation on your organization's culture, no matter how long it takes. It must be a culture with certain key values identified, communicated, rewarded, and nurtured.

And what are those key values? Trust, teamwork, and an ability to communicate, for starters. We strive to create a culture where there is appreciation for the effort that didn't quite make it, the so-called measured failure. We look to attract those that exude passion for going the extra mile, who understand the hot buttons of your customers, who have a wide range of interests, and who enjoy the process of collaborating for a common goal.

In the end, the success of your innovation implementation all boils down to a human resources issue. It is all about people. Your people. Who can pick up on how serious top management is about innovation and can tell if this latest effort will blow over in a year or two, or be in place in perpetuity.

Take Care of Yourself, Too

Let's face it, there will be a time when you feel overworked, overloaded, and overstressed. You'll put on a smile and tell your friends and family that you are fine. However, in your heart you know that you are drained from work. The phrase "drinking out of a fire hose" comes to mind. On top of it all, you are striving to turn the tide on corporate culture and sniping off innovation assassins.

Don't forget to take care of yourself.

This doesn't mean going to the gym once in a while or taking the odd family vacation. You need to take care of yourself intellectually, through undirected thinking. You need to find time to take a breath, and just . . . *think*. The idea is to let your mind wander, and create.

- Take the dog for a long walk after supper.
- Go for a drive, with no particular destination in mind. Just go!
- Read a book. Don't cheat—not an audio book. Read the book! It'll get your brain going, thinking about things other than the book itself.
- Keep a personal journal—just for you (no sharing). Even a paragraph now and then will help you sharpen your thinking.
- Take an hour off on your next long plane ride. Get a window seat and just stare at the clouds for a while.

THINK ABOUT:

- Does your organization suffer from analysis paralysis and, if so, what can you do about it?
- How are "creative failures" perceived and dealt with?
- Are innovation and operations bound tightly, or separated?
- How can you win over your organizational antibodies (or innovation assassins)?
- What forms of undirected thinking can help you both relax and sharpen your thinking?

CHAPTER 3

Master CEO-Speak

> Bureaucracy destroys initiative. There is little that
> bureaucrats hate more than innovation, especially
> innovation that produces better results than the
> old routines. Improvements always make those at
> the top of the heap look inept. Who enjoys
> appearing inept?
> —Frank Herbert, *Heretics of Dune*

A common lament heard at my Innovation Coach workshops goes something like this: "I only wish our CEO was like Steve Jobs. . . he'd 'get it.'"

(Actually, according to a *Fast Company* article a few years back, Jobs's default answer was "no.")

There are a great many talented innovators out there who share a common frustration with top management—the C-suite. The "suits." You've come to the right place, because I see the frustration from both sides: I am an innovation advocate and facilitator and yes, my current corporate title is president and CEO.

I'm here to help you master CEO-speak.

On one side of the aisle are the innovative women and men with stars in their eyes—and frustration in their hearts.

They see the positive attributes of their most senior leaders, for sure. These denizens of the C-suite are hardworking, visionary, determined, take-charge, keenly analytical, driven executives who—I have been told by the disenchanted—can have a hard time pulling the trigger on a new direction or a refreshing innovation. The disenchanted innovators I hear from boldly give their presentations—which are loaded with facts, figures, and details—see the heads in the room nodding, seemingly, in agreement, and then (they tell me, mystified) . . . *nothing happens.*

If innovation is so important, so desired, then why aren't the new directions we've proposed and researched acted upon? That's what I am often asked during conference breakout sessions, by people representing all sorts of organizations, small and large, in the private and public sector. *Where is the follow-through?*

What Is CEO-Speak?

Quite simply, CEO-speak refers to the language of C-suite executives. Mastery of this language is a pathway into their hearts and minds. Your abilities in this area can mean the difference between a home run and a strikeout.

Where is the disconnect? Why are so many valid new directions—needed paths to innovation—caught on the C-suite shoals?

To find out more about the CEO mentality, I called several of my innovation-expert associates around the world. Here are just a few of their comments:

"Companies, especially publicly traded outfits, thrive on predictability—and leadership is punished for non-predictability." These are the words of Wayne L. Delker, PhD, senior vice president, chief innovation officer, the Clorox Company. He leads worldwide R&D for all of the company's products, provides technical and scientific guidance within the operating divisions and other staff functions, and leads Clorox's multifunctional innovation process for developing new products and improving existing products.

Prior to joining Clorox, Delker spent fourteen years with General Electric, where he served as general manager of Six Sigma Quality for GE Silicones and general manager of Technology for GE Silicones. He also worked for five years as a research chemist for Union Carbide. His PhD in chemistry is from Columbia University.

When he speaks, I listen. "You can lose a lot of sleep, going for innovation home runs," he says.

Adds another innovation advocate associate of mine, Frido Smulders, associate professor of Product Innovation & Entrepreneurship and project leader of the Master's Honors Program, Delft (The Netherlands) University of Technology, "CEOs, by their nature, can be risk-averse. They need to manage risk because, in many instances, the risk inherent in innovation is tied to shareholder value. It's the system. It's the mentality."

Paul Hobcraft, advisor on Innovation Transformation, based in Switzerland, concurs: "The organization's leader does not want risk. He or she wants to push predictability. Even companies such as Procter & Gamble—regarded as progressive—are hard-nosed about screening out uncertainty. Today, they look for companies that have already succeeded, to reduce front-end risk and the need for validation or concept-proving."

Avoid the Big "No"

CEOs are risk-averse. With that as a starting point, how can you best convince top management to support your innovation?

How can you avoid situations where you leave a conference room after a big presentation with the boss, muttering that the CEO "doesn't understand the validity of our idea" or "was distracted during our presentation" or, worse, that you sensed "it was DOA from the moment we came into the room."

Bear in mind the myriad forces at play in the world of the CEO. These leaders want to enhance shareholder value and are painstakingly focused on ROI. They must keep, retain, and grow their customer base. They want their companies to come out winners in today's hypercompetitive environment and they look for ways to increase sustainable profitability.

In terms of the big picture, C-level executives want organizational and personal success. They do not want to fail, nor do they want to be "shown up." They definitely don't want to place a large bet on the wrong program. I can clearly recall Herb Kohler (yes, *that* Herb Kohler) leading monthly NPD meetings and remaining extremely hands-on in all facets of design and product introductions. We knew that what was important to "the man" was definitely going to be important for us.

Here are just a few key factors to consider as you identify ways to increase your chances with the CEO.

Consider Your Timing: Timing, as they say, is everything. A program you've developed that is in congruence with current organizational imperatives can fare better than a four-star innovation that is not in line with objectives. When CEOs create a company vision, it is wise to either propose an innovation that sharpens that vision or craft an element of the program that demonstrably fits the CEO's paradigm, whatever it may be.

Suggestion: Hold the program until the timing is right, or find a way to refine your pet program so that it is in line with current business imperatives.

Another consideration regarding timing is your sensitivity to current financial circumstances. If your company has recently suffered budget "hits," it might be wise to assess whether your program would fare better by holding it a quarter, or until blue skies return to your company's financial picture.

Build Consensus: A key to success in selling-in the innovation is building organizational consensus well in advance. Having to "sell" the idea to the boss in a pressure-packed, one-shot presentation can reduce the odds in one's favor. With the many hot items on the CEOs' plates at any given time, their ability to absorb detail is diminished. Coupled with the inherent risk factors of innovations, it becomes far easier and far safer for them to "just say no."

One person (or one small group) should not have to do all the heavy lifting required to get a new innovation program through to fruition. An ideal method would be to gain executive sponsorship of the program, if you will.

Support for the program from a wide range of internal constituencies will gradually build an air of inevitability around it. The broader the support, the better the program can fare, as getting internal traction requires push from people in different functions throughout the organization. Each internal sponsor has to believe that the innovation will yield benefits and have a personal payoff. Without these sponsors, your work is so much more difficult.

Sometimes these sponsors are found in the ranks of those who have tried other solutions and have failed. They will see your program as their salvation. Others are innovation-oriented visionaries eager to piggyback on your program. In either case, the ideal sponsor has the internal juice to deliver the financial resources needed to make the program fly and to influence others in favor of your program.

Without building consensus and finding the right sponsor partners, even the best innovations can die far before commercialization. To-do lists are packed these days, and budgets are stretched to the max. Sponsors—the right sponsors, who have signed off on your program—can make it happen.

Remember, though, that it is not necessary to get complete, up-and-down commitment from key stakeholders, as nice as that might be. What you want to achieve is to create a sensibility, a sense of inevitability, that permits the project to move forward, unobstructed, and that protects you with an internal buffer zone. At this point, you are leading the charge, but in a sense, leading from behind—a tactic that works beautifully in the three-dimensional-chess, *Game of Thrones* environment of many organizations.

Communicate Clearly and Regularly: Optimizing the timing and securing the right internal sponsorship is only part of the battle. Once your comrades are signed up and ready to mobilize with you, keep the progress reports on the process coming. It actually may be less about the idea itself than the process—how you've aligned "it" with corporate goals and strategy. Invite your new internal stakeholders to gain an ownership interest in the program by inviting their participation when creating the completed plan. In time, the plan will take on a life of its own and can be carried forward on many fronts.

Manage Expectations: While you build internal consensus for your program and communicate regularly with your internal sponsor network, it is important to manage expectations and keep the hyperbole to a minimum. Initially, it's important to first show how your program works within the corporate strategic imperatives, without touting unrealistic metrics about revenue or market share. Stay realistic and, thus, believable.

Another consideration is program scope. Sure, it's risk/reward, but the larger the size of the program, the greater the scrutiny it will attract. Therefore, you may wish to phase your program into relatively digestible pieces.

As the excitement around your program builds, the desire to toot your horn can be tempting. You're an alpha personality and this pride is understandable.

However, it is wise at this point to refrain from big internal announcements, parties, or other forms of overt celebration. Not yet. Now is the time to "run silent, run deep." Play your hand close to the vest and choose instead to under-promise and over-deliver.

I like to use the metaphor of starting a campfire. Experienced campers first get their tinder ignited, then slowly add twigs, and gradually add larger pieces of wood as the intensity of the flame grows. Too much lumber too soon will suck the oxygen out of the fire and extinguish the flame in short order.

The Devil Can Sometimes *Be* the Details

You will, of course, have crunched the numbers to determine program viability and found that it passes muster. Great—but be sure, as you construct your presentation, that you do not capsize your innovation by drilling far too deep the first time out. What you want to avoid is PowerPoint paralysis, a malaise that bottlenecks otherwise worthy programs by going way too far into the weeds, thus strangling any chance that it might see the light of day. Keep to the topline overview, and explain its fit with corporate strategy.

Elements of CEO-Speak

Imagine that you're in the executive conference room, pitching your innovation to the CEO. How are you speaking? What are you saying? How long are you presenting?

Remember that your business leader has many obligations on his or her plate, plus a number of "crises of the month." Therefore, it is critical to keep these elements of CEO-speak in mind:

"KISS": Remember to "Keep It *Short*, Stupid." Hone your elevator pitch to a tight minute or two. Keep to the topline elements and refrain from overload of executional details. Then open the conversation to questions, where you can further develop your thoughts, without having to plow through a lengthy presentation with the lights narcotically dimmed.

Let me go even further: get to your point in the first sixty-seconds. Too short, you say? Sixty seconds is a very long time. As an exercise, when you watch tonight's evening news, time the typical segment. You'll be surprised how concise they actually are these days. With attention spans ever decreasing, shorter is generally better.

By quickly opening the meeting to questions, you can turn the tables a bit and try to elicit from your CEO information that can help strengthen the follow-up meeting.

Prior to the meeting, list—and have handy—the questions you'd like to ask of your CEO. You'll be surprised to learn how easily these men and women will respond to thoughtful, honest questions—making it easier for you to help convince them of the worth of your idea.

(Additionally, create a list of "tough questions" you'll likely receive, and formulate concise, non-defensive answers that tie back to corporate directives.)

The downfall of some CEO meetings is the preparation of hour-long decks that would be brilliant at a tactical meeting among peers but are misused in this instance. The purpose of a presentation is to summarize key ideas in a way that is informative and engaging. If you have a lot of data, extract the important pieces. Do not make your CEO presentation a data dump. This is the type of CEO presentation that leads to another very different sort of KISS. That is, the "kiss" of death.

What Would Jimmy Stewart Do?: Film legend Jimmy Stewart burnished a reputation as a down-to-earth straight shooter who spoke naturally, without artificiality. I suggest you channel your inner Jimmy Stewart when pitching your senior management.

After all, you know your area of expertise cold and in far greater detail than the person two or more rungs up the chain of command could possibly know it. Therefore, it is important to trim your presentation of jargon and make it easily understood by a person who is most concerned with big-picture themes and who has limited time—and a limited attention span.

Don't make it "simple." But do make sure it is straightforward, in alignment with company direction, and understandable.

There Is No *I* in *Team*: I have no doubt that you are a virtuoso—a brilliant presenter. Please do remember, however, that your objective is to sell-in your program. Your focus must remain on the innovation you are presenting and the person to whom you are presenting. Although your contact with the CEO may be limited and your time for self-selling short, it will be important to minimize the "me" aspect of your pitch and keep your audience's focus upon the idea, not the person. Frame your idea in the context of the business. Leave your ego behind.

State the purpose of your program and relate it immediately back to the company's strategic direction. Your idea, then, can more easily be internally supported, with reduced sense of risk and enhanced ability to obtain funding. Make it easy for them to say yes.

Furthermore, if prepared correctly, your pitch will deliver valuable information—something for your target audience to think about well after your presentation has concluded. If you can accomplish just that, the odds of your getting invited to return on future pitches improve, even if this particular idea gets torpedoed.

Master Class: Storytelling for Innovators

We touched upon the importance of the quick, focused elevator pitch in a world where attention spans are short.

What is the best way to create such a dynamic presentation opening? To find out more about the process, I asked Costas Papaikonomou, cofounder of Happen Group, who firmly believes that *storytelling* is the key to success and is, actually, "fuel for innovation."

By storytelling, he refers to the process that truly captivates the audience, opening the mind to new possibilities and different directions. In this way, your C-suite audience becomes locked into your vision and can see things from your perspective.

In conjunction with writer Leo Benedictus and stage performer Jonathan Grant, Papaikonomou created these initial storytelling tips.

Know Your Theme: Essentially, this presentation of yours is a communications exercise. You need crystal clarity on what it is that you want to say to this audience at this time in the company's history. Why this innovation? Why now? With this clarity of purpose, you will remain on point throughout your presentation.

Can you express your theme in *six words or less*? For headline writers, six words is the magic number. Know your headline before you begin.

Ensure Impact via the Introduction: The introduction is the key to drawing in the listener and making that person listen to the end. Create a sense of intrigue to ensure that the audience hangs on your every word.

Have Courage: Tell your audience something they are not expecting to hear. "Own" your story and make it something to remember—and share with others.

Keep the Active Voice: Maintain an active, rather than passive, voice in creating your innovation story. In an active sentence, the subject is doing the action. A straightforward example is the sentence "Steve loves Amy." Steve is the subject, and he is doing the action: he loves Amy, the object of the sentence.

Or, consider another example, the title of the song "I Heard It through the Grapevine." "I" is the subject, the one who is doing the action. "I" is hearing "it," the object of the sentence.

In **passive voice**, the target of the action gets promoted to the subject position. Instead of saying "Steve loves Amy," one would say "Amy is loved by Steve." The subject of the sentence becomes Amy, but she isn't doing anything. Rather, she is the recipient of Steve's love. The focus of the sentence has changed from Steve to Amy.

If you wanted to make the title of the classic R&B song passive, you would say "It Was Heard by Me Through the Grapevine," which is not such a catchy title anymore.

Quiet Is OK: New storytellers can get rattled by quiet in the audience. Quiet can be OK, even much more than just OK. Quiet means they are with you, listening, hanging on your words. You have them in your hands. It's a good thing.

Know and Read Your Audience: It is important to understand well ahead of time the likes and dislikes of your C-level audience. Do they have a sense of humor, or are they all business? Do they have any current personal issues that you should be aware of? Or are there any cultural considerations to take into account?

You should have the same insights into your C-level crowd as you would from a consumer immersion. This empowers you and arms you with critical information. What are their hopes, fears, and dreams? What do they want to hear from your story? What do they value? What is keeping them up at night these days? What does success look and feel like to them?

And, most important, why should they care about your innovation? Communicators who know what will inspire an audience are in a very powerful place, especially if they clearly demonstrate how their innovation is in alignment with the needs of the audience.

The answers to these questions can help you properly craft your presentation. If you're the storyteller you need to be, you will get the insights you need well in advance and weave this info into your presentation to create a powerful, compelling narrative.

I once had an American associate who gave a fun, informative, but rather rollicking presentation to high-level executives from Japan. It would have been a home run with senior executives from big-city America, but it went over like a lead balloon with this quiet, conservative group.

Script Your "Improv": Carefully script your opening remarks, and then practice your pitch to make sure it sounds completely off the cuff. No surprises, no verbal cul-de-sacs, no going off on a tangent allowed here, folks. A very good family friend, who rose up through the ranks to lead the world's largest and most prestigious art auction house, once told me, in all seriousness, "I prepare everything, including my 'ad libs.'" As a young man, I thought he was joking. He wasn't. He always nailed his pitch. Every. Single. Time.

Use Your "Chunk" Theory: Stick to a basic structure, which opens and then "chunks" your presentation into three separate and distinct sections, followed by a recap ("Tell 'em what you're going to say, tell 'em, then tell 'em what you told 'em," as an old boss of mine would say). Sticking to a basic structure gives you the confidence to demonstrate the proper and culturally appropriate level of enthusiasm for your innovation that will prove memorable and have the desired end result: the green light for funding your project.

Your story should have key elements. It is helpful to define a problem-solution scenario. Define the challenge that needs to be overcome. Then tell us how your innovation "solves" the problem, which answers the inevitable question: "So why am I telling you this?"

When in Doubt, Leave It Out: Did you forget something during your pitch? Remember, you are the only person in the room who knows what you've left out of your story. Don't worry about it. Rather, keep going and either leave it out completely, or include the omission in an appropriate spot, or in summation.

Why a "Story" vs. a "Presentation"?: We hear a story differently than we do a presentation of information. The story may contain virtually the same information as the presentation but is told in a manner that is an immersive experience for the listener. We hear a story and we latch onto descriptions, we wonder what will happen next. We are at the edge of our seat.

The story format activates and engages the brain in ways that link to visualization, context, and how things relate. Here's the good news for you, as a storyteller/communicator: our ability to retain information in these sections of the brain is nine times greater than that which addresses our analytical faculties.

When was the last time you begged to learn "what's next" during a typical PowerPoint presentation?

"At my company, Happen, we appreciate the power of telling a great story," Costas says. "Big ideas need stories that take audiences on a journey that changes how they think, feel, and act. Good stories are humanizing and help people connect on a more personal level. Storytelling is very much in our DNA, and being able to tell a good story is a very powerful and important skill."

This is not to say that the story process is silly or clownish. Not by any means. After all, no one buys from a clown.

But the key here is to structure the presentation in a way that distills it, makes it impactful and memorable, and makes the benefits of your program clear and focused.

When your story is completed, it will be an engaging and compelling case that will satisfy your CEO in terms of a positive response to:

Does it align with corporate objectives?
Will it be profitable?
Is it doable?
What problem(s) does it solve?
Will customers love it?

What is more, you will have taken steps to advance your cause throughout your organization, our topic in Chapter IV: Top Down, Bottom Up—How Do You Build Organizational Consensus around Innovation?

THINK ABOUT:

- What are the key hot buttons for your CEO?
- Is this the right moment to unveil your innovation to the CEO?
- Have you done enough to create pre-meeting consensus for your idea?
- What is your program elevator pitch and short headline (remember: no more than six words)?

CHAPTER

4

Top Down, Bottom Up

Innovation is the ability to convert
ideas into invoices.
—L. Duncan

You've mastered CEO-speak and you got your buy-in on your latest program from the powers that be. And yet, you feel as if you are single-handedly pulling your innovation forward. Somehow, it seems mired. You feel stymied, frustrated at every turn.

Does this scenario sound familiar?

It is another common lament heard at my Innovation Coach workshops. Innovation—which is not itself an object, but rather a key tool used to reach strategic objectives—can only succeed if the CEO can create the delicate chemistry that results in a "top-down, bottom-up" culture of innovation rich with initiatives, engagement, and participation that includes participants at all levels of the organization.

If you have come to the realization that building innovation culture is largely an HR issue, congratulations. You now understand the size and scope of the culture-building effort before you. A full-bore innovation culture change can take years, as your people get comfortable with the notion that "innovation" is not an "add-on" to their "regular" job.

Innovation, they must learn, is now an intrinsic part of their function.

That's what I mean when I say that the art of implementation requires integrated support, from the top down *and* the bottom up.

It is not easy to accomplish when you consider the power of middle-management resistance, which can freeze the most dynamic program in place. Symptoms of this resistance can take the form of resentment, resistance and handoff issues, poor execution, and more.

SURVEY CITES KEYS TO INNOVATION SUCCESS

According to the results of a McKinsey & Company global survey, successful executives use multiple organizational approaches to drive innovation—and rely heavily on C-level support. In fact, nearly two-thirds (62 percent) of the survey respondents reported broad innovation portfolios structured with more than one type of organizational model. Further, nearly half said they use separate innovation functions less than three years old. Eighty-six percent said the structure of their separate functions positively influences outcomes.

Based upon my experiences with companies of all sizes, I was not surprised to read that McKinsey survey respondents noted the "same perennial challenge": competition with short-term priorities and integration of the function's strategic objectives with the rest of the business.

Among the other findings of the McKinsey study:

- *Strategy:* At companies where innovation and strategy are integrated, the executives reporting were six times as likely to experience separate functions that effectively meet financial objectives.
- *Integration:* A mere one-third of respondents reported that their innovation structure is fully integrated into their outfit's corporate strategy, and almost half believe that this integration issue is one of their most formidable challenges.
- *C-Level Power:* Fifty-six percent of respondents identify C-level (and leadership) support as a key reason for success, second only to "clear strategic focus."

Breaking Down Barriers via Alignment

To successfully break down the barriers to innovation success, it's important to receive C-level support—*and* business unit buy-in. Business units must "own" the innovation function, and the business unit leadership must love innovation. Without that business unit push, you will experience the "big freeze" that comes with shared resources and alignment problems. "Unless the culture is in place, it's difficult to make progress on the innovation front," said Martin Curley, director of Intel Labs Europe.

Middle-management resistance can be effectively resolved by instituting a single, unified annual financial objective such as EBITDA (Earnings Before Interest, Taxes, Depreciation, and Amortization). This helps eliminate silo-based objectives or other "distractions" to the common cause. Further, it "inoculates" the middle group in a way that gets them more quickly acclimated to the fact that their "regular job" now includes innovation-related activity.

My second-favorite strategy is a 70 percent personal role objective and at least a 30 percent new product sales objective that is used as a universal bonus, or reward, system. I have found that more traditional objectives and reward systems stand in the way of a common objective and optimal new product execution.

The effort to win hearts and minds must also include training and coaching, creation of a structured repeatable process (SRP), regularly scheduled activities, such as ideation sessions, and NPD update meetings.

In addition, successful companies institute big innovation-oriented events, such as annual idea competitions and exciting off-campus creativity retreats. The idea is to operate, promote, and institutionalize the critical nature of innovation.

And because three key people can effectively push the behavior of five thousand, it is important to have a blue-ribbon group of C-level direct reports (e.g., Finance, R&D, Sales & Marketing) communicating in lockstep, speaking as one, with regard to innovation and related policies.

Clear Communication Is the Key

If HR issues are indeed a focus, we must first examine our communication devices to ensure that we are broadcasting consistent imperatives regarding the need to innovate.

Paul Hobcraft believes that successful innovation requires a common language to succeed. "Innovation thrives from knowledge," he said, "and you need to make sure this is allowed to flow."

To make these essential connections, leaders need to

communicate a shared understanding of innovation, one that underscores the importance of the common sense of purpose. In companies with several hundred, or even a thousand, employees, relatively few will have the chance to observe your senior team on a day-to-day basis. "It's a matter of building a common language of greater understanding, which unites the group around innovation," Hobcraft said. Providing a context for their innovation engagement provides a clearer shape and meaning. "You are laying out the conditions, criteria, and circumstances, giving innovation its foundations."

For Paul, it becomes a matter of getting your team to get a clear representation of the "big picture," in order for the group to efficiently move their innovation activity within the structures, processes, and systems.

If you give each person a sense of meaning and trust, then their energies become more directed and focused.

It all starts with communication of that commitment to innovation. No longer is it simply "business as usual." You are building something different and you are building it together— that's the core communication all parties must receive.

I spoke recently to an Apple employee about her job and her company's culture. She smiled sheepishly as she said, "Well, I drink the Kool-Aid, but I don't swallow."

And while that may have been amusing, it brings up a very serious point. The corporate culture you wish to project and nurture so that it blooms with innovation that will win the day for years to come *is not Kool-Aid*. It is not some sort of cultish, or momentary, or poisonous project du jour. It has to be real and believable. It has to be honest. Consistent. And it has to be permanent, "cascading from the top of the organization to align and bring innovation to life for all involved," Hobcraft said.

Alignment Creation in Today's Work Environment

We will more fully develop this topic in the chapters ahead, but at this juncture it is critical to at least acknowledge the changing workplace environment and the many ways that today's younger business colleagues approach their professional life. Failure to understand the forces now at work in the business world will distort all efforts to create the top-down, bottom-up alignment needed for successful innovation.

Key characteristics of this new breed are that they are more open to risk than their forebears. They are also the first all-digital generation and highly proficient in current technology and platforms. They enjoy creating and nurturing social groups. They are team players attuned to working toward a common goal.

Moreover, they are impatient with "traditional" workplace environments and chafe under conditions that veterans might consider "normal." Whereas in years past the organization's culture would shape the individual employees, today it is the value system of the individuals that, collectively, define the organization's style and mores.

In this environment, how can you best create an ecosystem that allows today's talent to flourish? Consider these steps:

- **Cross-Pollination:** Once a certain structure and rewards system is set up, the linkages within the structure must be constantly strengthened and nurtured. For optimal innovation, your organization must be a paradigm of communication, one that fosters intra-organizational idea exchange and collaboration. It is almost as if you need to hang a sign from the rafters, saying "Open for Innovation." Actually, some companies achieve this by creating a designated space, the innovation center. When you have a severe case of organizational silo-itis, a dedicated innovation center can help break down walls of resistance because it sends a message that there is a new way of doing business at your organization.

- **Potential vs. Expertise:** Which is the most important innovation team attribute, potential or expertise? Answer: both! With a new wave of applicants in today's job market, you'll want to select some candidates with potential as well as some with direct industry expertise. A skill set and specific experience is certainly appealing, especially as older employees retire or leave. The newcomers need some hand-holding from those with vast institutional knowledge. But workplace populations turn over and people come and go. As your organization's tonality changes, it is important to recruit from the ranks of today's younger risk takers—those with the personality to embrace change. The only constant in today's business world seems to be "change." You may find that those with less real-world experience but significant upside potential may prove to be valuable, out-of-the-box thinkers who can step to the plate as tomorrow's innovators and company leaders.

- **Time to Think:** In today's pressure-packed, 24/7 work environment, where people are connected to the mother ship even while on vacation, it is imperative to structure your environment in a way that permits thinking time. By that, I mean time specifically set aside for working on innovation, away from the daily thrum of your people's "day jobs." Whether you call it an off-campus retreat, or a "hackathon," or a Skunk

Works program, or a Festival of Ideas (as Accenture has done in the UK), the idea is to not only to permit, but to push your folks to move their innovation projects forward and give them the time they need to do it. Some outfits even shy away from specific times and dates for the innovation magic to happen. These are run by savvy leaders who understand the personality and mind-set of today's newer employees (and, again, we'll get into this in great detail in the chapters ahead). They are basically told: "As long as you do your job, we are not that concerned about when you do it." They are treated as adults, as trusted and respected individuals, and they are encouraged to put valuable time against their innovation projects.

- **Nibble the Edges:** If your organization is just now starting to make strides in innovation, you may wish to consider taking risks along the periphery of your core business, rather than diving right into the core competency areas. First, see how the alignments work in non-critical areas, as you would test a new color of paint on a corner area, not the most visible section of the room.

- **Failure *Is* an Option:** Innovation means risk, and risk means that sometimes one fails. Failure, therefore, must be tolerated. Sure, "fail fast and fail cheap." But, yes, failure can and will happen. Without that freedom to fail, the team's collective courage to push the status quo will quickly evaporate and freeze your innovation efforts.

HOW GEORGIA DEALS WITH
INNOVATION CULTURE

The common belief in some circles is that the US economy is decidedly service-sector oriented, and that "we don't make anything here anymore."

Well, (a) not true and (b) many municipalities and regional not-for-profit organizations are helping private industry design and implement top-down, bottom-up innovation strategies.

Let's first debunk the myth that we don't "make anything here anymore." Did you know that more than 70 percent of export goods from the US are manufactured products? Or that manufacturers contributed $1.87 trillion to the US economy in 2012, according to the National Association of Manufacturers? In other words, manufacturing in the US is big business and will continue to grow as manufacturers invest in greater innovation.

As home to more than ten thousand manufacturers, Georgia's manufacturing sector serves as a beacon of strength for the state's future economic growth. In fact, according to Atlanta's Hire Dynamics, the job postings in manufacturing have increased over the last three years in Georgia, specifically in the Atlanta and metro Atlanta areas. Today in Atlanta alone, there are nearly seventeen thousand manufacturing job postings. The state is enjoying a renaissance in manufacturing as companies bring jobs back onshore from overseas and seek out Georgia as a viable location for their plants.

Innovation and a focus on workplace culture is sweeping across Georgia manufacturers, as they diversify by introducing new product lines, improve process control, and innovate their workplace and operations to improve employee quality of life.

This initiative is being fueled by Next Generation Manufacturing, a nonprofit supporting the growth and development of manufacturing in the state of Georgia. The mission of Next Generation Manufacturing is to make Georgia manufacturing companies aware of the breadth of local services available to them, such as the Georgia Institute of Technology, the Technical College System of Georgia, the Georgia Association of Manufacturers, and Georgia Quick Start. By utilizing the resources available to them in Georgia, manufacturing companies will be able to realize the key to growth: innovation.

Next Generation Manufacturing highlights the experience of Georgia manufacturers such as E-Z-GO, Blue Bird, Caterpillar, and YKK Corporation of America. These organizations are proud of the innovation taking place within their plants and the difference it has made to their production, customers, and people.

HR is the foundation of the innovation implementation process and, as we have noted earlier, the success of any company starts with its people. Employee quality of life plays a big role in that success. For E-Z-GO, the leading manufacturer of golf carts, innovation was needed in the company's workplace to revitalize employees. E-Z-GO was faced with a dark, dingy workspace with outdated equipment and an unengaged workforce before 2005. "I would lay my body across the entrance before I'd let a customer see the plant," said Kevin Holleran, president of E-Z-GO, of the plant's conditions when he joined the company. Holleran and John Collins, vice president Integrated Supply Chain at E-Z-GO, discussed the specific actions taken to rectify the company's problems during a recent Next Generation Manufacturing event. Actions include a communications cadence with regularly scheduled meetings and daily pre shift communications, as well as an initiative to drive down knowledge, increase training, develop leaders, and reward excellence through a pay-for-performance program. E-Z-GO's innovative ideas have reengaged its associates, a step that has improved productivity and morale.

Blue Bird, the world's leading school bus, specialty bus, activity bus, and green bus manufacturer, is also innovating from the inside out. To date, the company has innovated internal operations and cut back on product offerings to provide more value to customers. According to Dave Whelan, senior vice president of Manufacturing and Quality at Blue Bird, following an internal survey of employees on quality of life, the company implemented a crew work schedule that allows Blue Bird to scale the workforce to meet demand for the very seasonal business. Under this structure, only two-thirds of the workforce work at any one time, and Friday and Saturday are reserved for overtime during peak seasons. This schedule prevents the company from mass hiring during the busiest times of the year and mass layoffs when demand slows.

Caterpillar is innovating its operations as well, increasing its focus on process control, straight-line lean manufacturing, and standardization, while bringing manufactured goods back into the US. In yet another instance of onshoring, the products that will soon be produced in Caterpillar's new Athens facility are currently being made in Japan, and, ultimately, 1,400 new jobs will be created at the facility. The Japanese plant will be re-purposed by the company so jobs will be staying there as well. This transition creates a challenge of quality for the company as they try to recreate the high-quality product produced in Ja-pan within the US. To achieve this, the company is innovating and introducing stringent process controls to guarantee stan-dardization across the entire organization. These innovations will guarantee that the quality of a Caterpillar product is not compromised regardless of where it's produced.

When YKK Corporation of America was faced with a changing garment industry they, too, had to innovate. The company diversified its product line to stay relevant in today's economy. The garment industry has been on the decline over the past few decades in the US, and today 98 percent of all gar-ments are imported into the country, a difficult pill to swallow for a company that produces zippers in the US. For example, in 1998 Levi had twenty-eight denim factories in the US; today that number has been reduced to zero. The same can be said for Wrangler/Lee. In 1999, there were thirty-one Wrangler/Lee denim factories in the US, and zero exist today. To con-tinue to grow, YKK innovated its product offerings, expanding the company to specialize in architectural products like the ProTek glazing system for hurricane resistant windows and thermal products that reduce energy costs.

Culture Is King

Whether innovating within the workplace, diversifying product lines, or improving operations, culture is the glue that holds it all together and makes innovation possible for these

Georgia-based manufacturers. Strong workplace culture unites a company and increases commitment to the company and its mission. As we noted earlier, "Culture eats strategy for lunch," and it's true. A company can innovate, invest in technology, and train employees all they want, but without a strong top-down, bottom-up culture you'd be missing an opportunity to strengthen your company from the inside out.

"Manufacturers using innovation strategies to compete in the marketplace, over low-cost strategies, have been found to have higher returns on sales of over 10 percent, and higher employee wages, according to a recent Georgia Manufacturing Survey," said Richard Kopelman, founder and chairman of Next Generation Manufacturing and CEO and managing partner of Habif, Arogeti & Wynne, LLP. "Innovation is the driver that will make manufacturing once again the backbone of the US economy. Manufacturers must continue to innovate and introduce new products and technologies into their plants while maintaining a focus on their people and workplace culture."

Do You Have a Whip?

My father always advised me not to discuss politics in polite company. So forgive me for bringing political terminology into the discussion of innovation implementation.

However, as an organization builds its top-down, bottom-up structure, a whip is surely needed. In political parlance, the whip is an official whose primary purpose is to ensure party discipline in a legislature. Whips are a party's "enforcers," who ensure that party members vote according to the official party policy. A whip's role is also to ensure that the elected representatives of their party are in attendance when important votes are taken. The usage comes from the hunting term "whipping in," i.e., preventing hounds from wandering away from the pack.

Your culture of innovation needs its whip. Depending on the size of your organization, you may even need several. Let's again examine the McKinsey study referenced earlier in this chapter, specifically an area of great concern.

Fully 35 percent of respondents have ten or fewer full-time employees dedicated to innovation. If this is a top C-level priority, why is this number so low? I discussed this with one of my innovation-oriented colleagues, Nicolas Bry, senior vice president of Orange, the mobile carrier of France Telecom.

Bry agreed that somewhere in the journey from "best intentions" to "implementation," innovation has many places to lose its way. Bry referenced Vijay Govindarajan, noted author, forward thinker, and Coxe Distinguished Professor at Dartmouth's Tuck School of Business. According to Bry, these innovation masters actually believe that even "the whip" needs a whip. Often, the CEO commits to the plan, selects the leader to lead the strategic experiment, and asks a member of the senior corporate staff to shepherd it. And then, "the CEO makes a big mistake: *the CEO moves on to other matters.*"

The CEO's misstep, he said, is "buying into the romance." The mistake is assuming that the company has already hurdled the most difficult barriers in the innovation journey by finding a great idea and a great leader. In reality, the larger challenges are still to come.

Practically speaking, these innovation gurus believe that strategic experiments face their stiffest resistance after they begin to germinate, take root, consume resources, and clash with the existing organization well after the idea generation stage.

"It's extremely rare to find someone who can overcome

both the long odds that face any strategic experiment and an organization that fights them at every turn," Govindarajan wrote. "Organizations are almost always more powerful than people. Further, corporations serious about building a capacity for strategic innovation cannot simply hope that they have a few intrapreneurs somewhere inside that can save the day on their own inspired initiative. They must re-examine how their organizations are constructed. Only through careful redesign can organizations excel at both efficiency and entrepreneurship."

Your whips, through their force of will—and the four key levers Bry believes in—can help pave the way to acceptance of a "new world order" within the organization and diminish the fear that a company can feel toward innovation. These levers include:

- Detachment of resources coming from the parent company
- Creation of a network of decision makers
- The investment of the parent company
- A portfolio that reflects shared innovation goals

Some innovation experts, such as author Edward Glassman, have gone so far as to develop internal structures to help organizations convert ideas into profitable innovations.

Spreading a culture of innovation through "idea-improvement programs" is definitely a good way to prepare innovation acceptance within the organization, Bry said. "But it takes time to shape, and requires a management involved in innovation. What can you do if your top management is not so much a strong believer in innovation, and you don't have time to build a widespread innovation culture?"

If this is the case, it's time to turn up the fire and make things uneasy in the status quo zone. "One needs to **create the necessity of change**, to make the organization feel so uncomfortable that it decides on its own to move. Dissatisfaction is an engine for change—it makes you want to change your situation," he said. "We have to design the meaning of innovation."

This is an interesting thread, and I pushed him further to explain. According to Bry, a first step is to identify particular indicators of dissatisfaction in various areas such as competitive threat, business opportunity, deregulation, benchmark, and customer feedback. "They show that if we keep on that trend, the organization will face serious trouble," Bry said.

Then, he suggested that the company illustrates to what extent the innovation is a solution that will make the organization improve with regard to the previous indicators—here is where we truly **design the meaning of the innovation**.

"To get your innovation accepted, the organization has to share naturally the feeling of aspiration," Bry said. It requires using the right gesture, with the minimum of strength and the maximum of fluency, smoothly. In the long run, continuous innovation leads to nonstop successive change management waves. "You better start practicing," he advised.

How Orange Did It

"At Orange, the mobile carrier of France Telecom, executives decided to create a separate entity to be their innovation engine," Bry said.

"Vijay Govindarajan tells us that innovation cannot happen inside the performance engine, so it requires a dedicated innovation team. Every time you start a new innovation initiative—which the performance engine cannot do because of its limits of reach—you are essentially creating a start-up company.

"Setting an innovation entity acting as a start-up is what we experienced at Orange with the creation of Orange Vallée. Orange Vallée was created in 2007 to 'identify, develop, and market innovative products and services within particularly **short lead times**. Orange Vallée's offer would complement the group's portfolio on the world's Internet, mobile telephony, and convergence markets.'"

The adventure has been going on for three years now, and one can draw the following lessons, according to Bry:

- "Orange Vallée has succeeded in **identifying many 'hot topics'** like music on demand or smart TV that have further enriched the group portfolio: it has developed prototypes and products enabling us to perform market tests; its mission as **a scout and a 'house for ideas'** has been completed.

- "In less than 2.5 years, Orange Vallée has **developed and launched a diversified range of products** and services like the tactile tablet Tabbee, simplified and enhanced the mobile address book ON, web service Memory Life to share your memories, Transmedia Lab dedicated to storytelling across media, leveraging on technology trans-media apps.

- "What has been more difficult to achieve is a **streamlined cooperation with the core company**;

a clear selection of links to develop collaboration has been missed, as well as **living connections with innovation decision makers and the support of a sponsor** for the dedicated entity.

- "We have not been very good either at building an effective innovation management and methodology:

  - Our innovation strategy and belief did not meet **some concrete shared goals** with our parent company;

  - The innovation **portfolio management** has not been very balanced between disruptive projects and quick wins, not very focused on a selected number of projects, and it did not show a clear intent that everyone could use as a basis for individual and team decisions;

  - **No innovation process** pairing open innovation with design thinking, user involvement, fast integration, prototyping and testing capabilities, and cross-functional management has been shared and implemented so as to define a relevant framework for all the innovation team.

"Deriving from Orange Vallée, from our personal experience in innovation, and from in-depth research through academic sources and fifteen case studies, we have since tried to optimize the architecture through designing a 'Rapid Innovation' model.

"We suggested a framework with three main guidelines:

1. Create a dedicated entity empowered for fast innovation: flexible, agile, open to new opportunities picked out from the 'innovation market'; it will be half cast, both 'inside and outside' the core company, so as to bring back the innovation value to the core;
2. Instill 'creative tension': creative tension is a framework for creativity that leverages an agile organization and accelerates creation and development of new products and an associated leadership platform. A culture of diversity, focus, specific goals, and **knowledge circulation** in short cycles are some key components of a creative tension framework;
3. "Align with innovation strategy, by developing ongoing coordination with the core company, forging persistent connections between innovators and mainstream operations, cultivating communication and collaboration skills. Endorse some core strategic priorities, so as to **engage** more fluently in new co-innovations, following a line of least resistance."

In relating Nico Bry's tale to you here, I hope to convey a key message: top down, bottom up is very necessary. And very difficult. The world's premier organizations have difficulty implementing such a structure. Yet they keep at it, because the end result is so very worth the effort.

In Review

There is a darn good reason why *innovation* is one of the biggest buzzwords in business these days. It is an international obsession, and given our global business outlook, it should be one.

The good news is that, in my own personal experience, employee trust of leadership's intentions around "this innovation thing" is growing stronger. For the most part, I see leaders taking the positive steps needed to get their program messages cascading throughout the organization. I see employees who are being included in critical projects and being asked their opinions and ideas—and this engages teams and inspires them to give more of themselves, well above and beyond the effort it takes to complete their "day jobs." This is extremely healthy.

However, as we have seen, all is far from perfect in organization land these days. In his fine book, *The Art of Engagement*, author Jim Haudan writes eloquently on the topic of employee angst, and his thinking ties right back to the need to set up a top-down, bottom-up structure for innovation. Note, for example, the titles of some of his chapters, such as:

> "I can't be engaged if I'm overwhelmed."
> "I can't be engaged if I don't get it."
> "I can't be engaged if I'm scared."
> "I can't be engaged if I don't see the big picture."
> "I can't be engaged if it's not mine."
> "I can't be engaged if my leaders don't face reality."

Think honestly about the way your team feels. As you do, remember that we all have insecurities, fears, and worries—from the C-suite on down. It is our responsibility, our charter, to communicate in a way that eliminates as much of this negativity—this barrier to engagement—as we possibly can. If we are successful, the rewards can be unlimited.

THINK ABOUT:

- How clear is your innovation-related communication program?
- Do your key innovation people have time to think about their innovation-related projects?
- And do they honestly feel free to fail?
- Who is your innovation whip?

CHAPTER 5

Build Your Innovation Team

Success consists of going from failure to failure
without loss of enthusiasm.
—Winston Churchill

Y ou realize that the art of implementation requires integrated support, from top down *and* bottom up. You understand the tremendous role that HR-related dynamics play in marshaling organization-wide support for your initiatives.

Now it's time to build—and pressure test—your innovation team.

Take off the rose-colored glasses and evaluate your people. Who do you have in terms of real "players"? Who do you need? And who do you *not* need?

Our first stop is Jay Forte, president and founder of TGZ Group. Forte said, "You want the best employees; you know your employees build or destroy your brand with your customers. So who is the right employee? And who are the ones who will add value and make a difference? How can you determine if they will be a good fit for the job, but that they also will fit in your culture?"

In many of today's workplaces, Forte explained, "employees no longer do the same things over and over; situations constantly change. Employees must be constantly thinking and assessing to determine the most effective, efficient, and profitable response in each situation they encounter. This is how they add value, create customer loyalty, and drive results. And since not everyone thinks the same, not everyone will be the right fit for the job."

Therefore, Forte said, "the hiring process must move away from a review of what candidates have done, to one that assesses how they think and what activates their passionate performance. This requires the talent-based interview and its new way of asking questions and assessing fit."

Think in terms of mix-and-match scenarios. Which combinations of employees will meld the best so that you are all rowing in one fluid direction?

The American Productivity & Quality Center (APQC) recently studied approaches to innovation team composition. This leading proponent of business benchmarking, best practices, and knowledge-management research looked carefully at the approach taken by the Mayo Clinic's Center for Innovation. Interestingly, the heritage of innovation at the Mayo Clinic runs deep, since the late 1800s, when Drs. William and Charles Mayo founded their medical practice around the then-innovative concept of "the integrated team practice." This model and others have been utilized by health-care organizations worldwide to improve health-care delivery.

The Center for Innovation, created in 2008, is rooted in human-centered design thinking. The leaders of the Mayo Clinic are in complete agreement with what we are discovering here, together: innovation doesn't happen by chance. They firmly believe that transforming innovative ideas into practical solutions demands process, discipline, and focus.

The Mayo Clinic Center for Innovation builds innovation teams with a specific combination of personality types. Think about how many people in your innovation team fit into these general profiles.

They include:

- **Visionary:** The big-picture person who sees the grand purpose and has the desire to create what *could* be— and *should* be
- **Generator:** The pusher—the person who gets the innovation project rolling
- **Iterator:** This is your idea machine who can take the original idea and shape it into a true innovation
- **Customer Anthropologist:** Here is your link between your company and the end user, the one who knows all the hot buttons
- **Tech Guru:** As the name implies, this is the person who can use technology to transform the innovation into a real thing
- **Producer:** Here is your traffic cop, or expeditor—the one who manages the flow of ideas and keeps things moving
- **Communicator:** This is the person who can distill the essence of the innovation and pump up the volume amongst those outside the team by amplifying chief benefits
- **Roadblock Remover:** This person does whatever it takes to clear away financial, organizational, and political barriers to success
- **Future Caster:** This person can see the future of the innovation and articulate its economic and social value

Getting the chemistry right, getting the right mix of humanity on the team so that the magic of your idea moves forward, against all odds—this can be a messy business, especially today, a time of economic pressure, a time when so-called wiser heads strive to marginalize messiness.

In my experience, it can be wise to build a team from a variety of departments to help ensure a palette of viewpoints, for the best fresh thinking.

Thomas Edison was able to see right to the heart of it when he said, "The greatest invention in the world is the mind of a child." Childhood is a time of tremendous, spewing creativity, which society gradually pushes out of us. Not everyone has the "magic" and—in today's Amazon.com, algorithm-driven world—sometimes it seems as if there is no place for serendipity.

Today, even Major League Baseball, a strange and wonderful game from America's pastoral past, is increasingly run by the quants—those proponents of Moneyball, where statistics rule the day and "gut feelings" are spurned.

Creativity is, by chance, unquantifiable, elusive, and, at times, frightening. Yet colleges try to teach it. Organizations strive to capture it. So how does one capture lightning in a bottle?

In a 1971 interview in *Rolling Stone* magazine, musician John Lennon discussed how the Beatles song "Nowhere Man" came about. "I remember I was just going through this paranoia, trying to write something, and nothing would come out, so I just lay down and tried not to write and then this came out, the whole thing came out, in one gulp."

Yes, how to teach that? What's the recipe? Is there one? In his landmark book *Adventures in the Screen Trade*, award-winning screenwriter William Goldman rails against studio heads who try to crunch the elements of a hit movie. If it's that easy, why do so many big-budget blockbusters fizzle at the box office?

In reality, he says, "Nobody knows anything . . . Not one person in the entire motion picture field knows for a certainty what's going to work. Every time out it's a guess and, if you're lucky, an educated one."

The same thing holds for the book-publishing business. The legacy publishing houses have a hard enough time sifting through manuscripts to find the gems, and along comes Amazon.com, with its megatons of metrics on what consumers want and don't want, and tries to produce its own content.

And what happens? Not much. Amazon has not gotten any traction in their push to become a serious content provider. They sure can sell books published by others, though. But making the magic, in-house, that's another story altogether.

CREATE A GENDER-NEUTRAL ENVIRONMENT

The Supreme Court may have reaffirmed that companies are people. I think we can all agree that companies are groups of individuals, perhaps even mini societies, if you will. In your quest to implement innovation via the creation of the optimal team, your mini society must attract and retain the best and brightest men *and* women.

There's been a lot of coverage of Sheryl Sandberg's bestseller, *Lean In*, which some critics deride as *Falling Over*. Love it or hate it, the book sparked discussion about workplace gender issues, which I'd like to touch upon briefly here.

I've seen too many talented and supremely inno-vative women marginalized in their place of work. In addition to the egregious dissimilarities in salary between genders, some organizations seem not to "hear" the voices of women. I've been to many a meeting where a female colleague's insightful contribution or recommendation sank without a trace, as the alpha males in the room spoke right over it. Not two minutes later, a male coworker would suggest the same idea. Everyone's eyes would light up, most failing to recognize the blunder right in front of their faces. However, the message is clear to the female employee: *Your voice has no weight here.*

Today's savvy innovators are creating an inclusive environment, one that welcomes the valuable contribu-tions of women and men, young and old (the last will be discussed at length in chapter VIII).

There is nothing complicated about building a gender-inclusive work environment. It takes (a) an awareness of the disparity and essential unfairness of the male-dominated status quo and (b) the heart to do something about it.

Fair gender policies benefit employees of both gen-ders, as an article in *Fast Company* recently reported. At the national level, *women earn only 77 percent* of what their male counterparts do.

Again, this is an issue that affects men *and* their wives, sisters, mothers, and daughters. It has financial repercussions and, as we learned in Chapter IV, Top Down, Bottom Up, it is also a cultural issue—and cul-ture can be tough to change.

No matter. When the tonality of the environment

is the "old boys' network" that makes professional women feel uncomfortable, when people at meetings cringe at tactless and insensitive remarks, it's not only sexist, unbecoming, and unprofessional. It is not productive or conducive to eliciting the best thinking from the women on the team.

Such behavior may not even be overt, as so many elements of workplace culture are subtle reminders, rather than overt acts of sexism.

Ask yourself, what are the little messages or cues your team drops that might remind a talented female contributor that her thinking is discounted, or worse, not of any value at all?

Ask yourself, are younger females supported or mentored in a way that enables them to grow professionally and rise up the ladder?

Kathleen Davis for *Fast Company* puts it aptly: "Everyone loves to tout their innovative thinking and disruptive businesses, but how innovative or disruptive can you really be when all of your perspectives come from the same group of people?"

It should infuriate you when the excellent ideas of a colleague are stolen, co-opted, or ignored completely due to gender. Imagine your reaction if such behavior targeted a loved one of yours.

Here is the crux of it: Respect. As innovation leaders, we must make sure that the contributions from both genders are respected. In many offices, women's voices are undermined in subtle ways that must be addressed. The word gets out to recruiters and via social media, and your efforts to build an innovation team are slowly crippled as potential superstars look elsewhere for positions and inside talent leaves for greener pastures, to escape this ongoing marginalization.

I'd like to note, with great interest, the line in the *Fast Company* article that boldly proclaims that "one in ten women in the US is starting or running her own company and that these women entrepreneurs are three times happier than women who work for someone else." What does that tell us about the need to fine-tune (or do a ground-up renovation on) company culture, especially when women decamp from places where their ideas are not heard?

When you have a corporate culture that is gender-neutral, you give yourself access to the entire talent pool. You put yourself in position to attract and retain the best talent the market has to offer. If you don't do it, you bet your competitors will.

Let's strive to find the best and brightest people—*people*—who are "impact players," and together let's pledge to do whatever it takes to retain them. Do you know what innovation implementation boils down to? Simply put, it is the ability to find and retain the right innovators and to collaborate effectively with them. Leveraging your human capital should be a priority.

With so many working adults—men and women—entering the workforce on a global scale, imagine what can be done if this aggregation of knowledge assets is properly harnessed.

End of sermon.

An Elaboration on Collaboration

Let's elaborate on the topic of collaboration, because it is central to the nuts and bolts of building an innovation team.

Collaboration leads to optimal performance outcomes. Successful collaboration depends upon being able to marshal the forces of your innovation collective. And bear in mind that people are different. Sometimes very different. This diversity of backgrounds and work styles can result in exciting new perspectives and viewpoints that result in moving the innovation needle.

To foster collaboration, the innovation leader must be a skilled people person, one who is able to forge connections between team members to maximize results. Further, the team leader needs to constantly reinforce the innovation mind-set and the commitment to this philosophy.

A huge mistake I see in my professional experience and in my consulting work is that some well-meaning leaders of innovation dip in and out of the world of innovation in the mistaken belief that one can turn that culture on and off like a lightbulb. Trust me—it is not going to happen. A recent article in the *Wall Street Journal*, "Together We Innovate," discussed the need for team members to work in harmony in order to generate ideas. "Most companies continue to assume that innovation comes from individual genius, or, at best, small sequestered teams that vanish from sight and then return with big ideas." Actually, the article states, "most innovations are created through networks—groups of people working in concert."

Yes, with a variety of personality types, as outlined already.

The common denominator, however, is a passion for exploring new possibilities. You need to select a group that is committed and brave, willing to take on this challenge (now that you've given them "permission to fail" and encouraged them—all of them—to participate fully).

Again, let me stress the interrelationship between innovation implementation and culture management, which are two sides to the same coin. Building a successful innovation team requires relentless reinforcement of the "entrepreneurial mindset." How does that happen? Think about these leadership tips, which I've compiled in my decades of building and managing global innovation teams:

1. Encourage New Perspectives

Keep the dialogue open. Platforms for internal and external speakers can keep the thinking fresh and vigorous and get the creative juices flowing. Where to hold them? Central areas, to get maximum visibility: company atriums, lobbies, cafeterias, etc.

2. Link Your Thinkers

Deliberately reach out to experts from a wide range of company departments and connect them. This can be accomplished via the company intranet or in a workspace easily accessible to all departments. Note that Google simply hung an "ideas board" on a wall in a high-traffic hallway, and it reportedly has sparked innovative, anyone-can-jump-in solutions to thorny problems. There is value in merging the brainpower of people from all walks of professional life.

3. "Trust Your Stuff"

This is a baseball phrase used to help focus, or "center," pitchers who are overthinking in a particular situation. They are reminded to trust their ingrained skills—mechanics and techniques—and eliminate the extraneous mental noise.

Similarly, innovation requires the leader to encourage each member of the team to let go of the political "noise" and trust themselves (their "stuff") enough to trust each other. When you can accomplish this trust, you become more patient, a better listener, and, over time, more open—and productive—in the new culture of innovation being formed. That is when the real collaboration begins to germinate. Think of collaboration as taking leaps of faith together to discover new ways of thinking and creating superior results.

4. Communicate, Communicate, Communicate

If it is said that that three keys to success in real estate are "location, location, and location," the equivalent in innovation implementation is communication, communication communication.

Without consistent and regular communication, teams are not in synch. They find it difficult to build trust and collaborate. The manner in which you—as the innovation implementation leader—communicate establishes the structure and tonality that propels thinking and leads to new innovations.

5. Have Courage

"What do they got that I haven't got?" sings the Cowardly Lion in the classic motion picture *The Wizard of Oz*.

"Courage!!!" the Lion concludes.

For teams to innovate, leaders must challenge each team member to think outside their collective comfort zones, and think critically, in order to pierce the haze that clouds the path to success. No doubt, this can be a forbidding process that requires, yes, courage.

As the innovation leader, you must be the catalyst and crusader, who takes charge, embraces the role of a change agent, and pushes for the culture that, while disruptive in the short term, ultimately improves performance.

Such a role is admittedly not for everyone, for it requires fortitude and, at times, extreme risk taking. For those with the right stuff of entrepreneurial spirit, however, being that change agent can be well worth the challenge. And trust me, even if you feel that it is not your nature to be that person, you can, and must, grow into that role over time. It becomes second nature.

6. Check Your Organizational Chart

Organizations need a well-defined chain of command. Yet hierarchies can be innovation killers. Why? What happens when an innovative idea is hatched in the mid to lower levels of a given hierarchy? The ideas, as we well know, must sift—slowly—through the management morass, where they are tortured, twisted, and vetoed into the dustbin of history. There are a variety of reasons for this, including that old standby "not invented here" (territoriality). Vanderbilt professor David Owens has called this phenomenon a "hierarchy of no."

Interestingly, researchers have actually identified a cognitive bias against new, innovative ideas.

7. Don't Beat Yourself Up . . .

. . . if it takes time to get that ideal combination of people on your team. Trial and error rules the day, which is frustrating to you hard-chargers out there but is a fact of life. We are, after all, dealing with people, and this requires a sensitive touch on the tiller. Periodic course corrections are a predictable necessity.

Each reconfiguration of the team, or course correction, gets you closer and closer to the ideal chemistry and culture for your organization. It takes time, patience, and, again, courage to get to the point where you have an elite squad of women and men ready and eager to tackle the road to innovation implementation.

What About Dealing with Creative People?

So we agree on the need for collaboration, and yet some of you—I am sure—give pause at the notion of working with "those creative types."

In the first *Robert's Rules of Innovation*, one of the passages that got the most input from readers was the section in chapter V that discussed "the care and feeding of creatives." Oh those creative types! The typical stereotype is of the deadline-resistant dreamer, forgetful, with a faraway, thousand-yard stare, impossible to deal with, the redheaded stepchild of your team. And then, voila, they thankfully—and profitably—come up with the solution to the problem that no one else on your innovation team could have solved.

Based on the response of some of you, collaboration with the so-called creatives is considered a necessary evil.

In this chapter, which addresses the philosophy of building and "pressure-testing" your innovation team, I pose this question to you:

If a person with an Einstein mind was available to you, would you hire that person?

Have you read the great biography of Albert Einstein by Walter Isaacson, *Einstein: His Life and Universe*? Einstein had great curiosity and imagination—he was incredibly creative. But he was quite unlike a practical thinker such as Benjamin Franklin. Isaacson's characterization of the man is that of a "light-beam rider." That is, rather than obsess about mathematical equations, he would actually visualize himself riding alongside a light wave.

© Yousuf Karsh

In fact, he was rebellious and pushed back, hard, against authority, as evidenced by his political views and personal life. Einstein thought differently. He was more instinctive than inventors such as Franklin.

He was, however, a whiz in math, unlike popular wisdom about Einstein. And that underscores a fabulous insight about the man. He was a true left brain–right brain thinker. (Roger Sperry won the Nobel Prize in 1981 for his work on what is now commonly known as right brain–left brain thinking. Sperry theorized that some very specific activities are controlled by one side of the human brain or the other. The right side, he posited, controls creative tasks, while the left side is the domain of logic, language, and reasoning.)

In a brilliant essay by Patrick Ross, "A Creativity Lesson from Albert Einstein," Ross explains that Einstein's approach to problem solving began with big-picture thinking and creating abstract parameters to the problem at hand. At that point, he would use advanced mathematics to prove his theory. Ross's position is that Einstein's ability to start with big-picture thinking was only possible because he had such an exceptional foundation in mathematics (a left-brain activity). He was a left brain–right brain thinker—balanced.

The conclusion here is that the best creativity emanates from a balanced approach to thinking—*but the process can begin with whatever is easier or more comfortable for the individual.* There is no right way or wrong way to create, in other words. Some highly creative individuals prefer to work from a detailed outline, or blueprint. This guideline device helps keep some on track, even as details are altered on the fly. Others feel that the outline approach is confining. They'd rather "follow their muse."

It takes all types.

Many organizations and managers understand and accept this, intellectually, and yet still are resistant to the inclusion of the true creative type. I have worked with organizations that freely admit that things have to change, and I hear, "What we need is more creativity." They hire the people they need to help take them to the next level, and then they routinely beat the creativity right out of them, with processes that systematically destroy their ability to work with the reckless abandon that will yield superior results. These organizations do nothing more than pay lip service to creativity. Others are worse: the ideas are rejected out of hand, or publicly ridiculed, in favor of the tried and true.

Then the innovators quickly decamp for organizations that truly appreciate their ability to deliver. They are resilient and strong in the knowledge that they're different. After all, rejection of their ideas and their MO oftentimes began during the school days for such thinkers.

I see this with such frequency that I ask myself—and now pose the question to you: Does anyone even want—I mean, *really* want—creativity?

For some, I suppose, *creativity*—like *innovation*—is a buzzword du jour. There is really no long-term commitment to it. The consultants come in, sell-in their programs, create a slogan that serves as a corporate "strategy" (Ha! "The Road Ahead" indeed), collect their fees, and depart. And what's left behind are fancy binders and lost opportunities.

Why? Why are creative people, and creativity itself, admired and coveted, yet so often rejected out of hand? My personal feeling is that the answer is fear. Creativity: not everyone has it—and that makes it scary to some.

Creatives: they do not conform to convention, and—like the idealized person in the Churchill quote earlier—they persist, relentlessly, keeping at it, fully absorbed in their work, even to the exclusion of their personal needs. It takes guts to embrace innovation and its wellspring, creativity. To the less secure, the need for innovation and creative people seems to imply that they have done things wrong and that there has been failure, and blame to be affixed.

The plain reality is that most folks are risk averse and creative types are risk takers. Burying creatives in too much process is as bad as expecting or demanding creativity from those who just don't have it. Creativity can be fostered, or encouraged, but the plain truth is that some of us just don't have that ability, and it's cruel to expect us to deliver on something that is out of our reach.

To collaborate effectively with the creative people you need, innovation leaders must be willing to let down their guard and accommodate those who have a different set of skills, values, and way of working. If you can find, recruit, and land the right creative type for you, fear not. Consider yourself lucky. They are just what you need.

This all comes back to the culture aspect of innovation implementation that I referenced earlier. The corporate echo chamber, where everyone speaks in the same voice? That is an innovation buster, not the path to success. Rather than make the safe choices, the organization intent on ratcheting up the innovation must embrace new thinking, perspectives, and types of people.

Those people you recruit into your innovation team must be given the freedom to push back against the status quo, without fear of retribution. This freedom unleashes their capacity and helps get you where you want to be: industry leaders, rather than followers.

But here are a few unvarnished truths of the matter. Not everyone is creative (and there is nothing wrong with that). Not all organizations can handle the cultural upheaval that creativity/innovation brings. There is a price to be paid. And, finally, let us not put a value judgment on an organization's decision. Some will gladly pay the price to get the innovation it needs to survive. Others will opt for the safe, commonsensical status quo. To each his own.

But if you're reading this book, my sense is that you will embrace the creative personalities, warts and all.

How It Is Done: Two Real-Life Examples

If you *talk the talk*, you have to *walk the walk*. How are some companies actually going about building and pressure testing their innovation teams? Here are a few interesting examples:

Rite-Solutions (Middletown, Rhode Island): Rite-Solutions is a software engineering and IT solutions firm that seems to get the notion of innovation implementation through building an organization-wide culture. Here, creativity and innovation go far beyond technology and into the very fabric of the corporate culture. Management established a collaborative game that allows all employees to engage and have a voice in what technologies the company will pursue—and where they can be best applied. Financial and administrative functions are automated through smart-agent software and collaborative tools. Even corporate management is aligned through an innovative organizational concept that is community-based, not stuck in a hierarchical box. The result has been the growth of an innovative company—as opposed to a company that uses innovative technologies. Customers appreciate the value added, which is the bottom line.

Everyone in their organization receives $10,000 worth of virtual currency to invest in the company's internal "idea stock market." Employees can propose an idea, which is listed as a "stock" at $10 per share. Each stock is assigned a ticker symbol, and then idea champions encourage investment in their issue. A prospectus (actually called an "Expect Us") describes the idea and its potential. It's more than a cute idea. Employees are volunteering their time and expertise, and ideas that get traction are actually funded and developed. At that time, investors share in the proceeds through bonuses and/or actual stock options.

Does it work? In its first year of operation, the idea stock market accounted for 50 percent of the company's growth through new business. Plus, the innovation process cuts across hierarchical lines and, therefore, has been democratized, while keeping the chain of command very much in place.

Electrolux (Sweden): Global appliance leader Electrolux teaches by example. This company is the second-largest global appliance supplier, behind Whirlpool. The company sells products branded as Frigidaire, Molteni, and AEG, and their Grand Cuisine Line offers high-end kitchen appliances.

Carol Matlack from BusinessWeek.com provides some insight into Electrolux's transition from "being a capital-intensive organization to trying to be a talent-intensive organization." You will see how the company used a 360-degree approach to involve people from a variety of internal expertise areas in order to develop a breakthrough product design.

Step 1: Generating New Ideas

Matlack writes: "What is the most unpleasant thing about vacuuming? Swedish appliance maker Electrolux has a lot riding on the answer. So, two years ago, the company's market researchers spent hours in homes in Australia, France, and Russia, watching and asking questions as people vacuumed, then cataloging the 'pain points.'"

Here is a moment of truth for you: when is the last time you used your product or service? Many innovations and product and service improvements can originate from this effort. The company instructed its people to look obsessively for product improvements, easier assembly, better packing, a better service experience.

Step 2: Screening the Idea

Said Matlack: "Bag-less vacuum cleaners are rapidly gaining

market share globally, and Electrolux wanted to introduce a model that would stand out from competitors such as Dyson and Hoover."

Electrolux asked several customers what they felt were the most annoying things about vacuuming. Their researchers then spent hours observing homeowners vacuuming their carpets and recording their findings. These briefs were then turned over to designers for modification ideas.

Step 3: Testing the Concept

"The company tests potential designs with focus groups. Anything with a less than 70 percent approval rating is deemed not ready for prime time." The company's design was originally a modification to an existing vacuum created by research and development after studying some of the more unpleasant characteristics of existing vacuums.

Step 4: Business Analytics

"The R&D side of the triangle weighed in next, assessing the pros and cons of different approaches. For example, a motorized compactor would be more powerful than a manual piston, but would be more expensive and require batteries. In the end, the manual compressor won."

R&D became involved in the new product development process only after two rounds of focus groups were conducted with potential consumers. The first priority of the company was to find out what customers wanted in a vacuum.

Innovation should not be just R&D's responsibility; all should be involved, from customer to sales, finance, customer service, and operations.

Step 5: Beta/Marketability Tests
"The company tests potential designs with focus groups. Anything with a less than 70 percent approval rating is deemed not ready for prime time."

Electrolux went through three separate rounds of focus groups: one before design and two after initial designs to ensure the winner, termed the UltraCaptic model, was a vacuum cleaner that consumers wanted.

Step 6: Technicalities + Product Development
"Before settling on a final design, Electrolux convened additional focus groups to review the alternatives, pitting them against models offered by rival companies, with brand names concealed. The 70 percent rule was applied at each stage."

What about the Role of Your CINO?
The chief innovation officer, or CINO, is the person primarily responsible for managing the process of innovation. Innovation executives are often the facilitator of change and the leaders responsible for the development of corporate innovation culture.

I am a firm believer that the CEO must take the role of chief innovation officer, but in larger corporations, it pays to have a CINO who works and drives innovation on a daily basis. Due to the fact that innovation is not always immediately tangible, it is important to continually reevaluate the role and adapt to change in order to stay relevant.

Every successful business leader knows that innovation in business is essential, but the best way to engineer and sustain it is not always clear.

At a recent innovation summit, Luis Solis, president of Imaginatik, highlighted four essential steps to strengthen the

CINO position. These steps not only affirm the ten imperatives of innovation as originally outlined in *Robert's Rules of Innovation*, but they bolster my belief that successful innovation requires many different elements if the company is to cross the finish line ahead of the competition.

According to Solis, the best way to ensure that the role of the CINO does not follow that of the dodo bird (or, for that matter, the CKO, or chief knowledge officer) is to:

- **Make Innovation Imperative:** Language is crucial. Innovation cannot be an option, it must be a priority.
- **Show the Impact of Innovation:** Visible indicators of success need not only be monetary; your return on innovation can be changes in speed to market, patents, shortened cycles, and other measures. Remember that what gets measured gets done. Look for leading and lagging indications of innovations as written about before.
- **Investment in People and Time:** Educate your CFO about investing in innovation, so that you can invest in the people and time needed to make innovation happen. Create a culture around innovation. Educate and inspire.
- **Secure Institutional Trust:** Stakeholders in your business must understand that innovation is a shared win. Your corporate culture must also take into account that without risk, there can be no innovation. Use failure as a learning opportunity.

Building a solid innovation team requires a 360-degree commitment. "Innovation" must be more than a slogan. It must be interwoven into your organization's cultural fabric.

Further, all innovation efforts need to be cross-referenced with your organization's marketing communications efforts. Internal and external communications—including public relations—should reflect your orientation and initiatives, and underscore milestone achievements.

The bottom line: less talk and sloganeering and more effort to build a deep innovation capability with a systemic, holistic approach. It takes patience, resources, and commitment. But once you put the necessary drivers in place, you have gone a long way toward making your corporate innovation system sustainable—with a team that knows that you are not fooling around.

THINK ABOUT:

- Does your innovation team include a variety of profile types?
- Can you honestly say your team is gender-neutral? Can you attract and retain creative types?
- How easy has your organization made it to collaborate? Is communication ongoing and clear?
- Does your innovation team embrace innovation as you do, for the long haul?

CHAPTER

Ideate. Align. Repeat.

Microsoft is always two years
away from failure.
—Bill Gates

Your innovation team is built. You took special care to ensure that your dedicated team has the "right stuff": it's been carefully crafted, with a mix of veterans and newcomers, and the culture is vibrant.

You're ready to innovate for the long haul, yet you ask: how can we build this to last, and avoid being, in the parlance of old-time, Top 40 radio, a "one-hit wonder"? That is, the type of band that has one blockbuster hit and then sinks without a trace, never to be heard from again.

For us to create and sustain innovation, we must build a structured, repeatable process. Ideate. Align. Repeat.

That's the struggle, and for good reason. Let's take a look at the challenges and their solutions, from a variety of angles.

Eight Steps to New Product Development

Now that you've successfully woven the ten imperatives at the core of Robert's Rules of Innovation into the fabric of your organization, it is time to drill down a bit deeper. When teams collaborate in developing new innovations, having the following eight steps mixed into your team's new product development repertoire will ensure that its overall marketability will happen relatively quickly and accurately—and will enhance productivity across the board.

Step 1: Generating

Utilizing basic internal and external SWOT (strengths, weaknesses, opportunities, threats) analyses, as well as current marketing trends, one can distance oneself from the competition by generating ideas that take affordability, ROI, and widespread distribution costs into account.

Lean, mean, and scalable are the key points to keep in mind. During the NPD process, keep the system nimble and use flexible discretion over which activities are executed. You may want to develop multiple versions of your road map scaled to suit different types and risk levels of projects. We'll delve deeper into ideation later in this chapter.

Step 2: Screening the Idea

Wichita, Kansas, has more aviation industry than most other states. Here, innovations are booming, thanks to step 2: Screening. That is, do you go/not go? The idea is to set specific criteria for ideas that should be continued or dropped. Stick to the agreed-upon criteria so lesser-quality projects can be sent back to the idea hopper (or wood-chipper!) early on.

Prescreening product ideas entails taking your top three competitors' new innovations into account, identifying how much market share they're chomping up, exploring what benefits end consumers could expect, etc.

Step 3: Testing the Concept

As the economist Gaurav Akrani has said, "Concept testing is done after idea screening." And, it is important to note, it is different from test marketing.

Aside from patent research, design due diligence, and other legalities involved with new product development, knowing where the marketing messages will work best is often the biggest part of testing the concept. Does the consumer understand, need, or want the product or service?

Step 4: Business Analytics

During the new product development process, build a system of metrics to monitor progress. Include input metrics, such as average time in each stage, as well as output metrics that measure the value of launched products, percentage of new product sales, and other figures that provide valuable feedback. It is important for an organization to be in agreement for these criteria and metrics.

Even if an idea doesn't turn into a commercialized product, keep it in the hopper, because it can prove to be a valuable asset for future products and a basis for learning and growth.

Step 5: Beta/Marketability Tests

Arranging private test groups, launching beta versions, and then forming test panels after the product or products have been tested will provide you with valuable information, allowing last minute improvements and tweaks. In addition, this will help generate buzz. Wordpress is becoming synonymous with beta testing, and it's effective. Thousands of programmers contribute code, millions test it, and, finally, even more download the completed end product.

Step 6: Technicalities and Product Development

Provided the technical aspects can be perfected without alterations to post-beta products, heading toward a smooth step 7 is imminent.

According to economist Akrani, in this step, "The production department will make plans to produce the product. The marketing department will make plans to distribute the product. The finance department will provide the finance for introducing the new product."

As an example, in manufacturing, the process before sending technical specs to machinery involves printing MSDS sheets, a requirement for retaining an ISO 9001 certification (the organizational structure, procedures, processes, and resources needed to implement quality management).

In Internet jargon, honing the technicalities after beta testing involves final database preparations, estimation of server resources, and planning automated logistics. Be sure to have your technicalities in line when moving forward.

Step 7: Commercialization

At this stage, your new product developments have gone mainstream, consumers are purchasing your good or service, and technical support consistently monitors progress. Keeping your distribution pipelines loaded with product is an integral part of this process too, as one prefers not to give physical (or perpetual) shelf space to competition. Refreshing advertisements and impactful public relations efforts conducted during this stage will keep your product's name firmly top-of-mind among consumers in the contemplation stage of purchase.

Step 8: Post-Launch Review and Perfect Pricing
Once the product is launched, it is critical to look for ways to improve upon it. Most new products are introduced with introductory pricing, and final prices are nailed down after consumers have "gotten in." In this last stage, you'll gauge overall value relative to COGS (cost of goods sold), making sure internal costs aren't overshadowing new product profits. You continuously differentiate consumer needs as your products age, forecast profits, and improve delivery process whether physical or digital products are being perpetuated.

Remember: The Process Is Ongoing
The entire new product development process may be formalized, yet it should be considered an ever-evolving testing platform and kept loose. Errors will be made, designs will get trashed, and losses could very well be recorded. Having your entire team synchronized will ensure the successful launch of goods or services, even if reinventing your own wheel. Productivity during product development can be achieved if, and only if, goals are clearly defined along the way and each process has contingencies clearly outlined on paper.

How loose is "loose"? As the author, consultant, and educator at NHTV Breda University of Applied Sciences in the Netherlands, Soren Kaplan explained, "In the past, new products and technologies consumed the vast majority of the innovation airtime. That's no longer the case."

According to Kaplan, "The most innovative companies today realize that competitive differentiation comes as much from *how* they innovate as it does from *what* they're innovating."

As you consider ways to fine-tune your NPD process, Kaplan offered these five trends shaping today's world of innovation:

1. Cocreate with Customers

The convergence of platforms across the Internet, mobile devices, and social networking has created an environment in which customers play a more important role than ever. "Companies now realize that innovation is a team sport in which their customers need to play a direct, if not lead, role," he said.

Vans, a shoe brand with great appeal amongst a younger demographic, provides a fully customizable shoe-building experience on their website. "Customers literally start out with a blank canvas and design dream shoes that they can share with friends and family," Kaplan said. More and more, customer co-creation will be seen as one of the best sources of creating what customers really want—because customers create it for themselves.

2. Create an Experience

"You know that design has found its place when Fortune 500 companies like Samsung, Ford, P&G, and others instill chief creative officers and chief design officers to lead their innovation efforts," Kaplan said. Once upon a time, "design" used to connote industrial design. Nowadays, its scope has expanded to include experience design, he said. "Experience design involves the practice of designing products, services, events, and environments with an emphasis on the quality of the customer experience, not simply on form or functionality," Kaplan said.

Unilever, he noted, recently spun off an experimental retail store it created called Rituals. The store isn't organized by rows of products, but rather the personal "wellness" experience. Product names, colors, packaging, and promotion are all geared toward the consumer's desired emotional state and include areas focused on "relaxing," "energizing," and "purifying."

"Experience innovation provides a broader lens with which to view customers' needs and desires, which can help pinpoint the touch points that will deliver true surprise and delight," Kaplan explained.

3. "Servicize"

Services now account for about 80 percent of US output (GDP) and more than 70 percent of output from other industrialized nations.

Companies like Facebook, Square, OpenTable, and others have proven that great service business models can be built upon web and mobile technologies. "But as I described in a recent *Fast Company* article, 'servicizing' is as much about reinventing a product-based business model as it is about creating new services," Kaplan said.

Rolls-Royce, he noted, sells more than cars; they also sell airplane engines. When they modified their sales model and introduced service fees based on "uptime" (the actual time the engines are flying in the air), their airline customers were elated. "Airlines prefer to pay as their own cash comes in from their passengers and cargo instead of buying an engine up front," Kaplan said, adding that "Rolls-Royce sells 'hot air out of the back of the engine,' not the actual engines."

Servicizing, then, really represents a new way of thinking about customers and the value they desire, as opposed to supporting existing products.

4. Profit for the Greater Good

Today, a growing number of business leaders are attuned to a variety of environmental, economic, and social factors and are doing something about it. "Business should be able to make money while at the same time provide a broader benefit to people, the community, and the environment," Kaplan said.

This goes far beyond the Ben & Jerry's model, he added. Walmart, he noted, gathered more than one thousand leading suppliers to review goals and expectations for creating a more environmentally and socially responsible global supply chain. And "schools like Oxford, Cornell University, and Dartmouth College are creating a host of programs to help students create businesses that support the triple bottom line (people, planet, and profit)," Kaplan said.

Profit and purpose are no longer mutually exclusive. They're becoming intertwined as a source of competitive advantage.

5. Build Your Innovation Network

Open innovation and open business models will continue to drive new opportunities using external networks. More and more, the job of innovation has expanded to include employees, customers, partners, and anyone else who has value to contribute.

Here's a cool example: Kimberly-Clark's Huggies Mom Inspired program solicits new business ideas directly from "mom-preneurs." The company also promotes one-day "expert acceleration sessions" that bring hand-picked outside thought leaders face-to-face with business teams to foster fresh thinking and new strategies that can move the needle.

On this matter, the net takeaway is that how we innovate needs innovative approaches as well. It's not just the goods and services that need a new wrinkle in order to retain relevance. The innovation process itself can use a "refresh" or even a "gut rehab" every now and then, if the culture of innovation within our organization is to be sustained for the long term.

THE RAPID INNOVATION MODEL

One method employed by some savvy organizations is a revved-up, nontraditional approach to innovation: the rapid innovation model.

I have found that the linearity of processes such as the Stage-Gate model works very well. But I would be remiss if I did not present alternative methodologies, especially after taking the time to present the need for "innovative innovation."

Let's turn again to Nicolas Bry, senior vice president, Innovation, Orange Vallée. He is a proponent of rapid innovation. As the name implies, this approach is all about accelerating the innovation process.

Here's what Nico had to say in a recent conversation:

Is Modular Design the Key to Rapid Innovation?

In recent years, many firms have sped up their innovation processes, seeking to set up a rapid innovation model. But can we protect the meaning and relevance of innovation while accelerating and increasing its impact? This is exactly the issue challenged by component innovation.

Does Innovation Follow a Particular Model?

During the last twenty years, the linear process of innovation has been abandoned in favor of innovation by interactions, leading to new forms of organization. Innovation management positions have been created in order to define attractive and groundbreaking innovation lines, as well as encourage innovation culture within firms.

New organizations encounter change-management issues. Innovation can be considered as the creation of a new tradition: before being accepted and recognized, disruptive innovations change the values promoted by management, the payment models, the value chain. They even alter the firm's identity. Besides, these transformations take time and do not respond to the urgent need to speed innovation.

One might be greatly tempted to rely on models. A review of the most innovating firms offers many examples. Of course, as noted ironically by Dr. Gary P. Hamel, the American management expert and founder of Strategos, an international management consulting firm based in Chicago, innovation leaders unfortunately tend to disappear from the top ten from one year to another. And another question can be raised: can these models be replicated?

Let's take the example of Apple, one of the firms most regularly referred to in recent years. Not without reason: the implementation of an ecosystem that unites a terminal with services and contents, the search for meaning, at the crossroads of technologies, customs, and culture, relying on a strong design and on intensive marketing (conceived as an investment and not as a cost), a strategic management of its supply chain to keep a step ahead in assembling technologies—all of these reasons are examples that can serve as guidelines.

And yet, the company's CEO also plays a great role. Steve Jobs's idea was to keep a limited portfolio of innovations, a bold and remarkably courageous strategy that's difficult to imitate, as the common sense tends to aim at more diversified portfolios to share risks. The problem raised by Apple is basically; how to imitate talent. Many frogs have aspired to become an ox: they soon burst. If innovation is a search for identity, singularity is an inspiration but not a model of innovation. "Become the innovator that you are," as the great philosopher Friedrich Nietzsche would put it.

What Else Can You Say about the Rapid Innovation Model and Its Limits?

Keeping all these difficulties in mind, a new innovation model can be designed, with features taken from different firms and different contexts. This model aims for rapid innovation by relying on the autonomy and agility of entities dedicated to "creative tension."

The concept of *agile and autonomous* entities is easily understandable. That of *creative tension* is less obvious but is just as essential. It gives to the innovation team a focus, an ambitious goal: in a word, it leads the team to build a belief.

Rapid Innovation Model

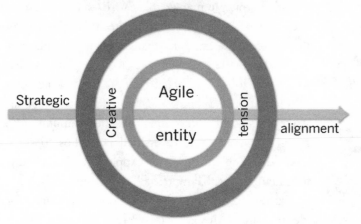

THCreativity, Inc. /nbry.com/rapid-innovation-model

To help organize the design work, it offers a creative framework including open innovation and design thinking features, combined with a user-centered approach, with a search for meaningful, fast, and iterative prototyping of lead-user design. The rugby approach used in the software industry and the model of circulating knowledge (metaphor, analogy, and model) conceived by professor Ikujiro Nonaka* (Hitotsubashi University) are essential to this framework and the pillars of creativity.

---

*Nonaka speaks about how companies must adapt to fierce competition and develop speed and flexibility. To his way of thinking, there is new game in product development, which means moving from traditional sequential phases to a **"rugby approach,"** involving a multidisciplinary team in constant interaction, whose members work together from start to finish. The team practices iterative experimentation and overlaps across several phases. This approach is essential to a company seeking to develop new products quickly and flexibly.

One of the main issues of this approach is to develop a collective approach leading the team to build a meaningful identity. Innovate means "to change while staying who you truly are," as explained by Dr. Marc Giget, founder of a series of organizations studying innovation and the impact of new technology on society. "Renew your identity while staying coherent with your culture" is the equation for the innovation team to solve.

But an innovation team still needs to convince its partners within the firm: the acceptance of innovation needs appropriation and commitment of teams and business units downstream. That cannot be done without aligning the innovation strategy with that of the parent company. The tools to build this alignment include a permanent dialogue with innovation deciders, granting resources, financial commitment of the parent firm in the project, and an innovation portfolio that brings into balance groundbreaking projects with probing projects and quick wins.

However, experience shows that this model also has drawbacks. To live up to its promise of a fast innovation, accepted and promoted by the heart of the firm, the three principles of autonomy, creative tension, and alignment are recommendations, though are not a guarantee.

The fact that these principles can be contradictory should not be overlooked—nothing really surprising, since the model itself is an attempt to resolve contradictions between the culture of innovation and the slower rhythm of big companies. Frictions are inevitable and arbitration is a delicate matter: for instance, working on an efficient alignment can lead an autonomous entity to share the creation process with the parent company, thus slowing down innovation speed.

Last, the setting up of innovation teams—focused on a challenge, united, and quite multidisciplinary—does not help the acquired knowledge to flow toward other projects and main business activities within the firm. That requires transversal management abilities and a strong desire to animate and share; in a word, altruism, which is a rare quality.

Should We Give Up on Rapid Innovation?

A well-documented approach offers a possible evolution: modular innovation, described by the Harvard Business School's K. B. Baldwin and C. Y. Clark at the beginning of the 2000s under the name modular design. This approach consists in breaking complex projects into separate modules that have as little dependence as possible and with precise interfaces. This independence helps improve a module by changing it for another or dividing it, with no impact on the rest of the modules. The substitution and division of innovating modules are vectors of value, as shown by Baldwin and Clark.

A successful application of modular design is open source. The management techniques for open source rely on the principles of modularity and distribution: a complex program is divided into multiple software components for which realization depends on the community.

The world of open-source software has developed remarkable tools for management: developing a collective identity, flowing knowledge through online networks, nonhierarchical governance, control, and command management based on initiative, but with a strict social control on the code's quality. Again, transversal management is crucial to gathering collective intelligence and achieving impressive innovation speeds.

Similar approaches include applications opening an operation window through an application programming interface (API) to third parties who will build an ecosystem, as well as intelligent objects sharing their data with developers who will create value by building services around these data. It is now a strong trend to conceive an application and simultaneously an API, or to develop an asset such as a telecommunication network through an API store.

Examples?

Instead of a complete application, materialized by an interface on a smartphone or on a television, we conceived a component, centered on one function that brings social and content together and connectable to multiple applications through an API: something like a hub, providing social TV data.

The first results are pretty good: half a dozen applications are connected to the social TV component and enhance the experience of Orange clients, helping them discover new content and increasing their loyalty to the brand.

In terms of conception, the benefits are significant. Nicolas Bry is a brilliant thinker, and that is a lot to digest. These questions imply technical and scientific views, but also a market approach. But in Nico's viewpoint, "We need to build complex solutions, dealing with the firm identity." Much more than just an organization issue, innovation management is a continuous process of improvement, building on the cyclic circulation of knowledge.

Ideation Clarification

Ask any team or group to define innovation. Behold, the "Rashomon Effect." That is, contradictory interpretations of the same event by different people. The phrase derives from the movie *Rashomon*, where four witnesses' accounts of a heinous crime are all different.

There are three basic levels of innovation:

- Incremental: Here we have the least risk/difficulty, and the lowest returns—along with the possibility of more innovations allowing you to keep pace in your industry without losing much sleep
- Transformational: With greater risk comes greater potential returns and the type of shift that can allow you to lead the market
- Breakthrough: The risks are highest, and so are the possible rewards, as the few-and-far-between breakthrough can allow you to shape new markets—and lose lots of sleep.

Types of Innovation

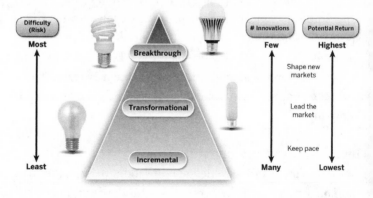

Copyright © 2014 Brands & Company, LLC.

Source: Brands & Company, LLC

In today's business environment, it is my belief that—rather than focus on the breakthroughs only—organizations might consider building a structured, repeatable process by starting with incremental advances, or line extensions. Breakthroughs can be added to the mix over time.

Actually, the type of innovation you consider can be broken down even finer, as this *Ten Types of Innovation* graphic demonstrates:

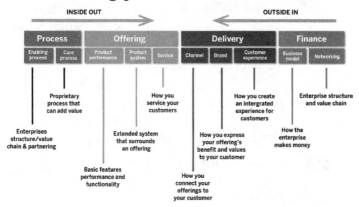

Source: Doblin On Innovation Effectiveness, March 2005

Source: Doblin Group

Here, we can see a way to spread the excitement and the responsibility among a variety of internal publics. Innovation is everyone's task. Every department must accept the challenge.

As for how to ideate, there are many methods—including those detailed in our first *Robert's Rules of Innovation* (chapter VII). These include both real and virtual world idea hoppers, such as:

- Internal Ideation Sessions: held regularly, or at least twice yearly; held off campus, facilitated by a third party and definitely not the boss (which would be inhibiting); include wide range of invitees, from Finance, Customer Service, Technical, etc.
- External Input: from customers, trade show surveillance, competitive intelligence, etc.; from focus groups and user groups
- Internal Online Suggestion Box: to allow ongoing additions to ideas
- Outside Innovation Platforms: investigate the use of companies such as Mindjet (formerly Spigot). Mindjet is a platform that has the capabilities to drive enterprise innovation at scale. It provides the framework needed to build sustainable, predictable, and repeatable innovation process. Organizations use such outfits to drive engagement that lasts and choose the best ideas with greater assurance, allowing validation of the investment you've made in your innovation.

Applied Concept Mapping

Innovation can be a messy business. You wrangle people, only to wrangle their ideas, searching for connections that may or may not exist.

Organizations need easily understood and curated methodologies to help share ideas across minds. That is where concept maps come into play. According to Brian Moon, knowledge management expert at YourEncore, Inc., concept maps (Cmaps) are diagrammatic models based on theories of human learning and forty years of research. They were introduced in the 1990s as a solution for problem solving.

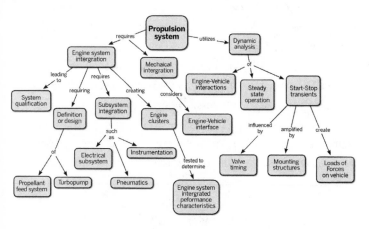

Cmap Applied concept
Source: THCreativity, Inc.

The Cmap helps organize the basic elements of the concept, with a logical flow that explicitly shows the relationships
between concepts, without limiting the viewer's imagination.
Cmaps effectively portray the most intricate, dynamic idea.
Thus, they are quite unlike the basic, if not downright clunky,
diagrams many of us commonly use in our PowerPoint presentations. The largest and most renowned multinationals in the
world regularly use Cmaps, up to and including P&G.

Alignment

While most organizations believe that innovation is required to
remain competitive in today's marketplace, they often do not
put enough emphasis on building the organizational *capability*
for innovation and aligning the processes with the needs of the
organization. Idea management is a critical step in this process.

While creativity and ideas can be found in numerous places
and in numerous ways, how you manage them determines the

viability of a product or process. Ideation should be harnessed by a process with dedicated resources, and with NPD and LTD teams working together.

According to Linda Hill, a professor at Harvard Business School, "Companies struggle to innovate because they do not know how to lead the process." By simply making small changes in the way you manage ideation, you create an organization that not only is *willing* to innovate, but has the *ability* to do so. Follow these helpful tips when nurturing creativity and managing the idea process.

- **The Rules of Engagement:** When meeting with your innovation team, clearly convey what you are looking for. Since this is sometimes too general, it is also important to outline what ideas you are not looking for. Provide the summary of the overall process and how ideas will be evaluated in this process. Purpose makes people willing to take risks and do the hard work inherent in any innovation process. Identify the need for continual improvement and what is required to implement the changes you need to succeed—and double-check your strategic alignment.

- **Protect Your Intellectual Property, and Beware Patent Trolls:** In the research and development industry where innovations build on top of other innovations, obtaining patents to protect your intellectual property is a large part of managing your ideas. Not only do patents protect newly developed products or processes, they contribute to unrealized value creation.

  A troubling trend gaining more exposure lately is the increase in patent trolls. Top patent licensing company Conversant Intellectual Property Management recently launched an educational campaign against the use of extortionist demand letters victimizing small- and medium-size businesses. Bad demand letters often sent by shell companies (trolls) are a big problem for US small businesses, costing them millions of dollars in settlement fees.

Our friends at Hoffman & Baron LLP, an excellent IP resource, remind us that legal protection today is even more important than it was when my first book was published in 2010. Competitors lie in wait around the world, and staying out of harm's way is critical. Working with a trusted and reputable IP law firm can prevent your company from stepping on another company's IP and protect your valuable trademarks and trade names against counterfeiting and other unauthorized uses.

Most important, strong protection of IP gives investors that warm and fuzzy feeling that makes good things happen for your firm.

- **Think "Diversity":** Innovation usually emerges when diverse people collaborate and share. When holding meetings, it is often advantageous to include other individuals in your organization that may not be part of your innovation team. This may include customer service representatives, sales team members, or even customers. Customers are often willing to offer input that represents the consumer side of innovation and can take some of the guesswork out of the question, "What does the consumer want?"

- **Shake Up the Norm:** To achieve a varied demographic, break up think teams into groups that may not normally work with each other. This can help to shift the normal "idea leader" into more of a supporting role, while giving a voice to others not normally involved in the innovation process. Constructive conflict can result in better solutions and ideas.

- **Boycott the Conference Room:** Never hold a meeting simply for the sake of holding a meeting. Dismiss unnecessary members or excuse team members when their talking points are finished. Variety is the spice of life. Meetings that follow the same format in the same location for the same number of minutes week after week can stifle the creative juices. Move an idea meeting into the break room or outside. Utilize agendas one week and free-form brainstorming the next.

- **Give out Gold Stars:** Creativity is sometimes a taxing intellectual process. Contributors must be recognized and rewarded. Employees that are supported are satisfied employees.

  Many employees crave the ability to create. Jason Kroskrity is the senior manager of the Chemistry and Electronics Laboratory for Mattel. He spoke about his career opportunities when studying epidemiology at UCLA: "The idea of not having a creative piece as part of my profession started to scare me," Kroskrity says. He left school and was recruited to Mattel by a high school friend in 1998. As described by *Forbes,* "Now in the lab where Slime was born forty years ago, Kroskrity and his team come up with the chemical components of toys, such as the cosmetic grade ink for a

Barbie digital nail printer that paints photos right onto
fingernails. One of his most recent projects to hit the
shelves is the Hot Wheels Car Maker that lets kids in-
ject melted wax into a car body mold. It passed muster
with a tough critic—Kroskrity's nephew."

- **The Idea Database:** Just like sales items and raw goods,
  ideas should be inventoried. Create an idea database
  and review it regularly. Some great ideas may have been
  created at the wrong time. Often a great idea is waiting
  for the right problem to come along.

Repeat

To build a sustainable culture of innovation, your organization
must develop a repeatable, scalable methodology. The momentum must continue over time.

This requires regular communications, updates, ideation
sessions, review meetings, and more, as we discussed earlier.

It must also be a subject on the monthly management
meeting agenda, just like finance. The monthly NPD meeting
should review all projects in the works, including a status update, next steps, and key milestones. Projects that do not pass
muster in your gates, do not deliver enough margin, or do not
prove to be technically feasible should be eliminated. Remember: fail fast and fail cheap.

Of course, new projects and assignments must be continuously added. Further, regular reprioritization of top projects
must be conducted as part of your overall portfolio management efforts. This reprioritization should take into consideration current needs, consumer demands, market dynamics,
and other key factors. Ideally, your team will always maintain
a grouping of top projects, ensuring that a sudden change in
priorities will be minimally disruptive.

THINK ABOUT:

- Do you currently utilize a gate process of some sort to help track your process?
- Have you tried rapid innovation in your efforts to fast-track ideation?
- Does your organization shoot for breakthrough, transformational, or incremental innovation?
- What steps have you taken to ensure that your organization will not become a one-hit wonder?

CHAPTER

Crowdsource Your Way to Innovation

*I am looking for a lot of people who have an infinite
capacity to not know what can't be done.*
—Henry Ford

Around the world, savvy leaders now employ crowdsourcing methodology to "harness the power of the many" in their
efforts to build sustainable innovation into their organizations.

Are you? And, perhaps more important, *should* you?

When Did It All Start?

The first mention I can recall of the term "crowdsourcing" was
by Jeff Howe in *Wired* magazine, back in 2006. The article referenced the pharmaceutical company Eli Lilly and its launch
of InnoCentive as a way to bring "external" innovative minds
into the conversation. Major multinational companies—Boeing, DuPont, P&G, and the like—post some of their most difficult scientific problems on the InnoCentive website, and the
network goes to work in order to develop a solution.

According to the aforementioned article, the heart of
crowdsourcing is in the diversity of intellectual background
among contributors. This idea is further strengthened by the
"Theory of Weak Ties" by Mark Granovetter, which was pub-

lished in the *American Journal of Sociology*. According to the theory, weak ties enable us to reach populations and audiences that are not accessible via strong ties. In the case of crowd-sourcing, the most efficient networks are those that link to the broadest range of information, knowledge, and experience.

There are many definitions available for crowdsourcing, but I think Jeff Howe said it best the first time. "Crowdsourcing represents the act of a company or institution taking a function once performed by employees and outsourcing it to an unde-fined (and generally large) network of people in the form of an open call."

Although it may seem as though crowdsourcing is the result of modern twenty-first-century methodology, the ba-sic premise has been around for centuries. For example, *The Oxford English Dictionary* started out in the late eighteenth century as an open appeal to collect idioms and phrases from thousands of volunteers around the world.

il Duomo
Source: iStock Images

Even earlier, according to Ross King in his book *Brunelleschi's Dome,* Florence's Wool Merchant Guild created several lucrative contests to help spur the creation of Italy's famous Santa Maria del Fiore (yes, il Duomo, as it is generally known). In the early 1400s, the guild designed its programs to attract the finest artisans in various trades needed for different parts of the church. They appealed to masons, carpenters, engineers, and sculptors (among many others). These contests overlapped in a magnificent project to build the world's widest dome.

As time has moved on, the Internet has facilitated the interactions behind crowdsourcing. Today, crowdsourcing and open-innovation websites allow people from all cultural, economic, and educational backgrounds to collaborate on groundbreaking technology.

Kickstarter may be the most famous example of an online crowdsourcing platform. Since its launch in 2009, it has grown to become the largest funding platform for creative projects, with more than 4.2 million people pledging in excess of $652 million to fund more than 43,000 projects, according to a recent article in the *Guardian.*

Open Innovation, Co-Creation, Crowdfunding, and Crowdsourcing—Compare and Contrast

Various principles and concepts are used for managing research and innovation. Organizations are gradually becoming more adventurous in their approaches to innovation. The innovation and idea-management company Wazoku explains three increasingly popular concepts. All three are complementary, yet they each reflect different applications of innovation and idea management. They are as follows: open innovation, co-creation, crowdfunding, and crowdsourcing.

Open Innovation: Open innovation, which we covered in detail in our first *Robert's Rules of Innovation*, means creating and innovating with external stakeholders: customers, suppliers, partners, and your wider community. Companies are increasingly seeking to work and source knowledge beyond their boundaries. Henry Chesbrough, the American organizational theorist and adjunct professor and executive director of the Center for Open Innovation at the Haas School of Business at the University of California, Berkeley, is known for coining the term *open innovation*. He defines it as "the use of purposive inflows and outflows of knowledge to accelerate innovation. With knowledge now widely distributed, companies cannot rely entirely on their own research, but should acquire inventions or intellectual property from other companies when it advances the business model . . . Competitive advantage now often comes from leveraging the discoveries of others. An 'open' approach to innovation leverages internal and external source of ideas."

According to the innovation consultants at Wazoku, open innovation creates an environment where individuals and organizations can actively get involved in the creation of mutually beneficial solutions. They believe that open-innovation decision making helps democratize problem solving and build collaborative community engagement. Open innovation, the experts at Wazoku say, is an inclusive, social way of solving complex issues and improving processes.

What about Co-creation? While open innovation suggests active collaboration between different organizations and the sharing of intellectual property, co-creation relates more specifically to the relationship between an organization and a defined group of its stakeholders, usually its customers. The most common definition is: "*An active, creative and social process, based on collaboration between producers and users that is initiated by the firm to generate value for customers.*" (C.K. Prahalad and Venkat Ramaswamy, "Co-Opting Customer Competence," *Harvard Business Review*, 2000). Co-creation means working with the end users of your product or service to exchange knowledge and resources, in order to deliver a personalized experience using the company's value proposition. While crowdsourcing is people creating a great idea for you, co-creation is about people working with you to make a good idea even better. Co-creation is also a way of enhancing customer engagement by directly involving them in the company's value creation and product-development processes.

Crowdfunding: Crowdfunding, which is collaborative funding, typically via the Internet, has grown exponentially over the past few years. There are currently hundreds of crowdfunding sites, including Indiegogo, Kickstarter, and RocketHub, that match people in need of capital for ideas, projects, businesses, and causes with investors who want to support them. Established banks are actually at risk of being bypassed as entrepreneurs and small businesses turn to crowdfunding to raise capital, according to the experts at Forrester. The threat most directly affects small-business lending, venture capital, and alternative investments.

Crowdsourcing: Crowdsourcing occurs when an organization outsources projects to the public. An organization decides to tap into the knowledge of a wider crowd, and input is sourced from a large and undefined group of people. Crowdsourcing requires a lower level of engagement and involvement than open innovation and co-creation. An organization using crowd-sourcing will set a challenge to the public and ask for opinions, insight, and suggestions. It is an open call to the public whereby the organization solicits solutions from the crowd—not genuine contribution and collaboration. Open innovation and co-creation imply a stronger involvement from the stakeholders who are included in the value and creation process.

From a business perspective, crowds are often more cost-effective per output or per worker than traditional company solutions. For start-up companies with limited resources, crowd-sourcing is a means of accessing funding, talent, and assets on a global scale. It also provides a chance for you to involve customers in the final product of your company, thus increasing buy-in before the product hits the market. Consider the story of Harley-Davidson from chapter II and its rollout of the Project LiveWire electric motorcycle.

According to the *Harvard Business Review* (Kevin Boudrea and Karim Lakhani, "Using the Crowd as an Innovation Partner"), "While companies are relatively well-coordinated environments for amassing and marshaling specialized knowledge to address problems and innovation opportunities . . . [a] well-functioning crowd is **loose and decentralized.** It exposes a problem to widely diverse individuals with varied skills, experience, and perspectives. And it can operate at a scale that exceeds even that of the biggest and most complex global corporation, bringing in many more individuals to focus on a given challenge."

In addition to benefits of scale and diversity, crowds offer incentives that companies may find difficult to match, the authors stated. These relate back to issues of territoriality and culture we addressed in earlier chapters. "Companies operate on traditional incentives—namely, salary and bonuses—and employees are assigned clearly delineated roles and specific responsibilities, which discourages them from seeking challenges outside their purview. But crowds, research shows, are energized by intrinsic motivations—such as the desire to learn—that are more likely to come into play when people decide for themselves what problems to attack."

The authors posit that the opportunity to burnish one's reputation among a large community of peers is another strong motivator (as is money, to be sure). Also, crowds are often more cost-effective per output or per worker than traditional company solutions. "The crowd has become a fixed institution available on demand," the authors conclude.

In my opinion, it is wise to be aware of such methodologies. I am not suggesting that one gives up on building your innovation culture from the inside out. However, looking externally to crowdsourcing and its many cousins may prove an interesting and exciting adjunct to your organization's current program.

Think of it as harnessing the expertise of a wide group of people to help solve problems. Think of it also as gaining the ability to mobilize a vast network to pitch in on key projects, as needed. Even for funding.

Then this incremental input gets integrated with your internal resources.

What Types of Organizations Use Crowdsourcing?

Many types of organizations now crowdsource regularly: from pharmaceutical houses, to mass market breweries, to restaurants, to book publishers, to municipalities. The most common reasons for getting in on the power of crowds include: reducing cost and overhead, increasing options (crowdsourcing delivers access to thousands of "helpers" across a wide range of experiences and cultures), optimizing creativity, and increasing buzz. On this last point, note that some platforms allow you to run surveys and voting through your social-media accounts, tapping your fans and your network to vote on solutions. Not only does this provide valuable feedback, it creates a perpetual buzz as the process continues.

Crowdsourcing and the B2B vs. B2C

I am asked in my consulting work how crowdsourcing works with B2B and B2C companies. In my experience, there are some factors to consider:

Differences:

I am one of the innovation people who believe that crowdsourcing works better for B2C companies. To me, this is because many B2B companies work less directly with consumers and end users. I have found that when the organization typically works directly with consumers and end users, this experience and mind-set fosters experimentation and open-mindedness.

Similarities:

They share many of the same issues and challenges. With both, the real work starts behind the scenes, and this goes for both types of companies. Even with access to fresh, new external input, you still have to integrate this into your organization in order to bring out better innovation. This is difficult and requires the intensive, ongoing culture building we discussed earlier. It is hard work.

Corporate innovation units in both types of companies share many of the issues and challenges we discussed earlier, including:

- Getting executives to buy into and commit to innovation
- Developing an innovation strategy
- Building a strong innovation culture
- Making business units engage in innovation
- Improving communication with regard to the corporate innovation capabilities
- Merging external and internal resources to create better innovation
- Moving beyond incremental innovation and bringing out more disruptive innovation

The approaches to these issues and challenges are quite similar regardless of the type of company. Overall, however, I find that more and more innovation happens through communities.

In my opinion, the future innovation winners will be those that manage to bring together current and potential innovation partners and create ecosystems and communities. The big challenge is how to make such communities work, and this goes for both B2B and B2C companies.

Challenge-driven innovation can help both types. Service providers such as NineSigma, InnoCentive, and IdeaConnection focus on challenge-driven innovation (which we'll explore in greater detail later in this chapter) in which they help companies (seekers) connect with individuals as well as other companies (solvers) in order to get their problems solved. Such an approach can be applied within many different kinds of business functions. Therefore, it can bring value to both types of companies.

Examples of Crowdsourcing

For purposes of illustration, let's take a look at how different types of organizations have utilized crowdsourcing methodologies.

Book Publishing: Imagine that you are a first-time author, proud of your work, and you learn that your publishing company lets fans vote on manuscripts and choose which ones are published.

According to a recent article in the *New York Times* (Alexandra Alter, "Publishers Turn to the Crowd to Find the Next Best Seller"), one author's publisher, which specializes in young adult fiction, had nearly nine thousand readers sample her story online, which drew the highest possible rating. Her publisher is planning a hefty first print run of 100,000 copies in the United States and simultaneous releases by its sister imprints in Britain and Australia. This is virtually unheard of for the work of a first-time author.

Yet Swoon Reads, part of Macmillan Publishing, "is upending the traditional discovery process by using crowdsourcing to select all its titles," the article stated. "By bringing a reality-television-style talent competition to its digital slush pile, the publisher is hoping to find potential best sellers that reflect not editors' tastes but the collective wisdom and whims of the crowd.

"The fans and the readers are more in touch with what can sell," said Jean Feiwel, senior vice president of the Macmillan Children's Publishing Group and publisher of Swoon Reads, who came up with the concept in 2012. "They're more at the pulse of these things than any of us can be."

The company's site has ten thousand registered users. Readers also vote on audiobook narrators after listening to digital audio samples, decide which cities the authors visit on their tours, and choose the books' covers.

Has publishing gone the way of *American Idol*? According to New York book-publishing contacts, this one publisher's approach reflects a new push by writers and publishers to build a fan base for books well before they are published—and sometimes before they are even written. By inverting the usual process of releasing a book first and finding an audience later, publishers are aiming to become more like the rest of the entertainment industry, where new TV shows and films are subjected to rigorous market testing before they are shown.

On Kickstarter, writers collectively raised $22 million last year in funding for some six thousand works in progress, which ranged from teenage novels and comics to nonfiction books.

Even some established best-selling authors are dipping their toes in the world of crowdsourcing. For his book *The Innovators*, Walter Isaacson posted a chapter on the website Medium to get readers' feedback and ideas about his central argument, namely that technological breakthroughs often come from collaboration rather than solo genius.

Another legacy publisher, Avon Romance, a division of HarperCollins Publishers, created a site for aspiring romance writers to share their novels and get feedback, in the hope that great new novels would surface. Editors scour the site every week to evaluate the manuscripts that are getting the most positive feedback.

Publishers and writers see crowdsourcing as a way to not only uncover new talent but also measure fans' reactions before a book even goes to press (see earlier: create buzz).

Restaurants: Once upon a time, in 2008, a DC restaurant named Elements was created, and it proved one of the most interesting examples of crowdsourcing.

It was an organic foods restaurant formed by a "beta community" of more than four hundred online members. The idea was to offset the biggest bugaboo of new business ventures: being undercapitalized.

According to an article in the *Washington Post*, the community estimated that it would take as much as $1.5 million to get the restaurant up and running. Community members would have a voice in the development of the restaurant and become part of its profit-sharing model, based on a point system.

The Elements crowdsourcing approach also gained it access to a four-hundred–person focus group, in essence, providing feedback on various executional facets of operations. The restaurant business is tough, and the management wanted to increase the odds of success.

In his great book *What Would Google Do?*, author Jeff Jarvis noted that a restaurant called Inscrutables launched in Amsterdam. It, too, was crowdsourced.

In such cases, whether or not you think crowdsourced restaurants are a bit gimmicky is perhaps beside the point. The idea is that young entrepreneurs are using technology to build communities to help them grow and build an outsized share of voice in their local markets.

Municipalities I: Brightidea, a leader in on-demand innovation management, helped Ireland foster its economic renewal efforts a few short years ago. The program was called Your Country, Your Call (YCYC). Brightidea's WebStorm solution helped the country collect, manage, and track ideas from across the land.

With Mary McAleese, the eighth president of Ireland, as its patron, this massive campaign was a countrywide, community-based action initiative to spur sustainable economic growth through citizen-based ideation and innovation. An award of €100,000 for each of the top two ideas was given, along with a development fund for implementation of up to €500,000 each project.

"Your Country, Your Call was about creating something that will make a long-term positive impact on the future of Ireland, its people, and its economy," said Austin Hogan, Ireland's YCYC program director. "The program provided a comprehensive tool set for managing and tracking ideas that was easily rolled out and customized to fit our particular needs."

YCYC had significant backing for an open-innovation challenge through traditional and nontraditional media. Not only was the competition designed to gather a large volume of proposals, but the overall campaign was structured with a detailed road map for funding and implementation of the two winning entries.

"The Irish people have a long and proud tradition of creativity. From the poems of William Butler Yeats to the invention of Boolean algebra—the very foundation of modern computer science—Irish ideas have changed the way the world sees and thinks," said Matthew Greeley, CEO of Brightidea. "For the first time, Ireland invited innovative proposals from anyone, anywhere. With such a tradition of creativity, it is only fitting that a movement such as this began in Ireland."

The competition was open to anyone with an idea for Irish development.

Municipalities II: Brightidea also worked with the City of San Francisco to help collect, prioritize, and manage cost-saving and revenue-generating ideas from its more than twenty-six thousandcity employees through ImproveSF.org. The results were incremental, to be sure, but the effort was noteworthy and the savings real, if not earth-shattering.

Ideas submitted through the innovation portal were evaluated by select department heads using Brightidea's Switchboard product. The top idea was selected for implementation with ten other high-ranking ideas recognized in an event with the mayor and cosponsored by the San Francisco Planning + Urban Research Association (SPUR) and the Municipal Fiscal Advisory Committee (MFAC), as well as featured on SFGov.org and the city's Facebook page.

"ImproveSF.org allowed the city to tap into valuable ideas from city employees to help solve some of our most pressing issues," said former mayor Gavin Newsom, who is now the lieutenant governor of California.

This open-innovation campaign built on the momentum created by the Open Gov Initiative for the City and County of San Francisco which focused on open data, open participation, and open source. It was the first of several campaigns designed to gather input from employees as well as citizens on some of the city's most pressing issues.

"The City of San Francisco has always been at the leading edge of many cultural and social movements," said Matt Greeley, CEO of Brightidea. "The Open Gov Initiative opened government processes and data to invite fresh thinking at all levels. This world-class program will be a model for many others around the globe."

"ImproveSF.org tapped into the knowledge and experience of our city employees to help solve some of our most critical financial issues," said Newsom. "The initiative and the winning ideas were part of a larger story on how government in partnership with its employees can encourage innovation. The ImproveSF.org program served as a tool for the city to encourage and collect ideas from its employees."

In a matter of weeks, there were seven hundred active participants, four thousand votes, and nearly seven hundred comments. Of the 569 total ideas submitted, four were chosen for immediate implementation. Many others were held for possible future savings or revenues. Winning ideas included:

- Eliminating hold music, for which the city was paying more than $900 per month
- Reducing washing of municipal vehicles, for which the city had paid $75,000 per year
- Allowing 311 to take credit card payments for selling city and MUNI merchandise
- Auctioning surplus and/or unwanted property and vehicles

The ImproveSF.org campaign builds on momentum created by the Open Gov Initiative for the City and County of San Francisco, which focuses on open data, open participation, and open source.

Public Relations Agencies: Ketchum, one of the largest public-relations agencies in the world, also used crowdsourcing platforms to power its thriving open-innovation platform, Mindfire.

Mindfire is Ketchum's proprietary online community platform that engages more than three hundred students from nearly thirty universities around the world to post ideas to creative challenges for top brands. Ketchum provides career opportunities and training to students who participate, and prizes are awarded when an idea is selected by a Ketchum client. More than fifty challenges have already been conducted through Mindfire, generating hundreds of valuable insights and creative idea starters for brands like Wendy's, Hertz, and Frito-Lay.

"Mindfire has been used for Ketchum clients from China to the UK to every major market in the US, generating new creative directions for our teams to consider in as little as twenty-four hours," said Karen Strauss, chief innovation officer at Ketchum. "With flexible, customizable software, we are able to manage a robust online community where imaginative contributors share solutions to expand our idea pipeline for clients," added Andy Roach, chief information officer at Ketchum and a codeveloper of Mindfire.

Ketchum activated several social features to create a private "Facebook-style" community, and the success of the agency's program has already led to its expansion to Asia, South America, and the Middle East.

While most agencies were still helping clients build fan pages and collect "likes," Ketchum's social network tapped into young talent from around the world—in a private setting—where creativity, innovation, and co-creation flourished.

Medical Facilities: Harvard Medical School utilized platform-based expertise to help find a faster, more accurate solution for a tool that calculates the edit distance between a query DNA string and the original DNA string. The medical school previously was able to process one hundred thousand sequences in two thousand seconds (thirty-three minutes, twenty seconds). HMS then dedicated for an entire year a full-time Harvard developer who reduced the computational time to four hundred seconds. With only $6,000 in prize money, 733 registrants and 122 platform-based experts submitted working algorithms. The winner provided HMS with a winning solution that clocked in at sixteen seconds.

HMS paid a fraction of the cost it would have paid to hire an IT consultant, as well as its own internally dedicated university resource (coder).

Crowdsourcing and You

American innovator Bill Joy, cofounder of Sun Microsystems, believes that "**no matter the enterprise for which you work, the smartest people in your field work for someone else.**"

The talent is everywhere—but how to find it? That is the question. Use of an open platform, with hundreds of thousands of community members, experts in their field, can allow your organization to tackle even the most complex problems.

This is at the core of the appeal of crowdsourcing.

Your company may very well pride itself on its proprietary NPD processes and core of internal collaborative prowess. Yet over the past few years, the fact is that a growing number of organizations have at least begun to experiment with opening up their strategy processes to those previously out of the loop when it came to strategic direction setting. Examples include 3M, Dutch insurer AEGON, global IT services provider HCL Technologies, Red Hat (the leading provider of Linux software), and defense contractor Rite-Solutions.

While such efforts are at different stages, executives at organizations that are experimenting with more participatory (or "inclusive") modes of strategy development cite two major benefits. One is improving the quality of strategy by calling for diverse, detailed new perspectives that had been overlooked but that can add greatly to the outcome.

The second is building enthusiasm and alignment behind a company's strategic direction—a critical component of long-term organizational health, effective execution, and strong financial performance. As I stated earlier, such collaboration requires hard work and culture change. And sometimes, time is of the essence.

Yes, there's that word again: *collaboration*. What does collaboration mean to you? Working together? OK, and what does *that* mean?

For me, true collaboration means a robust sharing of ideas and getting the most out of diverse ranges of skill sets and talents so that the whole is greater than the sum of the parts.

This is where crowdsourcing can be a plus. It simply opens the door wider, so that the task allocation can be spread across more minds, from diverse backgrounds, perhaps with perspectives that look down upon the forest, rather than with a point of view that is too far down "in the weeds."

As reported by Innovationexcellence.com's Cris Beswick, in a recent UK survey 75 percent of CEOs said *"fast-changing market conditions are forcing companies to reinvent themselves quicker than ever before."*

That, according to Beswick, "means organizations are going to have to figure out what the next 'iteration' of themselves needs to be and make plans to morph shape, structure and adapt in order to stay relevant. One major barrier is that 62 percent of business leaders admit it's 'almost impossible' to gain support to test and develop ideas. Unless that changes, the ability for organizations to innovate and move from the old game to the new game is at risk."

Let's face it. The business world is changing and we need to change with it.

But it takes courage to bring more people and ideas into strategic direction setting. Senior executives who launch such initiatives are essentially flexing their muscles to distribute power—as they must.

It takes courage, because in order to take these principles to their logical conclusion, leadership must adapt its role from omniscient decision makers, expected to know everything and tell others what to do, to "social architects," who spend time thinking about how to create the processes and incentives that unearth the best thinking and unleash the full potential of all who work at a company.

The CEO and other top executives are not pulling back from their roles. In fact, they still have the right, and the responsibility, to step in if things go off the track. And, as always, they continue to be responsible for making the difficult compromises that are always at the core of sound strategy.

But it also may be increasingly important for strategists to lead in different ways. For example, to convey the message that the contribution of employees is of vital importance, top executives should constantly confirm that it is and set the example themselves. This approach requires a more direct, personal, and empathetic exchange than the once-in-a-while town hall meeting allows.

For a mass digital dialogue to succeed, as I've said before, your people need to feel free to express themselves openly. This can be anxiety-producing.

Is Your Organization Ready to Crowdsource?

When it comes to crowdsourcing, therefore, an important element of leadership is honestly assessing the readiness of the organization to open up and stimulate engagement. This sounds simple, but overlooking it can be costly.

Source: THCreativity, Inc.

A McKinsey report recounts the tale of the leaders of one (unnamed) mutual insurance company who enthusiastically called upon its workforce to share reflections on an innovative, soon-to-be-launched life insurance product. Despite the leaders' expectation that the open call would generate a torrent of endorsements, it was met with the sound of crickets. The silence was deafening.

"Closer inspection revealed that people were acutely aware of the strategic importance that senior management attached to this innovation," the report stated. "And nobody wanted to wreck the party by openly sharing the prevailing doubts, which were widespread. The doubts proved well-founded: within a few months of being launched, the new product was declared a failure and shelved."

Freedom to fail, freedom to be negative. This McKinsey story is a cautionary tale that points to a key element of strategic leadership.

That is, how to encourage dissent without fear of retribution. Enabling employees to communicate through ambient signals instead of relying on words and elaborated opinions is an effective way to lower the threshold and still catch the prevailing mood. Familiar examples of ambient dialogue include polls, "liking," and voting—simple functions that allow participants to express an opinion without being exposed. More powerful and sophisticated forms of ambient dialogue include prediction markets (small-scale electronic markets that tie payoffs to measurable future events) and swarming (the visually aggregated representation of the emergent mood or motion within an organization).

Consider how a prediction market might have helped the mutual insurer. The opening market quotation for the new life insurance product would probably have taken a steep dive, revealing the negative assessment of the internal market. This would have immediately alerted managers to potential weaknesses, without exposing the employees who had the courage to reveal the problems.

While these are still early days for social strategy, I believe that it holds tremendous promise to enhance the quality of dialogue, improve decision making, and boost organizational alignment to create sustainable innovation.

But yes, it takes real courage.

The Grand Challenge Contest

A grand challenge is a formula for successfully finding such solutions by inviting the world's best minds to apply their technical or scientific talent to the problem or opportunity at hand. The winning providers go back to their research labs or workplaces with prizes that may be in the millions of dollars along with the knowledge that their solutions are one step closer to implementation.

Key to meeting program expectations is identifying the right grand challenge topic in the first place. It doesn't have to be a lofty concept filled with noble promise, meaning the CEO doesn't have to commit to eradicating poverty from the face of the Earth. It can be a practical challenge such as creating an easy-to-install water pump for developing countries. Or a challenge that is critical to solving an even bigger challenge—for example, fighting malaria in third-world countries.

What the topic should be is relevant to the sponsoring organization's industry so that it is easy to link its importance and success to the company's brand. And it should be doable. In other words, the challenge should be able to generate a sufficient number of concepts and potentially viable solutions that it accelerates progress and is therefore worthy of the prize money and media attention.

Pursuing a grand challenge not only requires a deep technical understanding of what a successful solution must do but also confidence in the worldwide technical community's ability to come up with it. This confidence can only come from knowledge of the industry as well as insight into who is currently working on state-of-the-art technologies related to the challenge—from the sponsoring organization's industry as well as other sectors. Moreover, third-party grand challenge companies understand how to take a complicated initiative with many moving parts and manage it from inception all the way through proposal evaluation and the selection of winning submissions. In their role as challenge producers, they are critical to ensuring the initiative is credible and wins the respect of stakeholders, solvers, and the press.

A successful grand challenge requires a close collaboration between technology and marketing experts. It should be guided by a program design that specifies the goals of the challenge, the "need statement," a web-based outreach strategy to the worldwide community of solvers, and a marketing plan for generating awareness and recognition for the sponsor from kickoff through the award phase.

We did just such a program in my days at Airspray International, when I created the formulation challenge. This was a worldwide call for entries from formulators, who were challenged to find new formulas compatible with our innovative one-touch mechanical foamers, used in personal-care and household products. The results were astounding, and the resulting public-relations boost helped further advance awareness of our firm and our product range.

A tightly managed media campaign is a critical factor for achieving recognition as a visionary organization. Marketing and public-relations experts know how to frame the grand challenge for greatest media impact, how to ensure the sponsoring organization gets the credit for it, and how to keep the

Source: Rexam Airspray, B.V.

grand challenge fresh and newsworthy after the initial intro-ductory buzz. A successful grand challenge also respects the technical community asked to solve it. While technologists and scientists understand the higher societal value of a grand challenge and want to be part of real change and progress, they are quickly alienated by insincere efforts.

Although prize money is surely welcome, it is sometimes a secondary consideration. Equally valued are recognition for their advancement and a home for a solution or technology that they've worked hard to develop.

Additional "rewards" are the potential interactions with business advisors, funders, peer technologists, and scientists, or sponsoring organizations that a grand challenge may spark.

A company skilled at managing grand challenges knows how to clearly articulate a grand challenge's need statement, technical requirements, and performance expectations in a way that respects the priorities of potential solvers and gets them excited about ap-plying their experience and brainpower to the problem.

Naturally, one of the first questions a CEO asks about a grand challenge is: "How much does it cost? Why is it worth an investment of millions of dollars?" Bear in mind that the prize money varies depending on many factors, including the perceived "size" of the challenge and its long-term societal val-ue, the breadth of the challenge topic, the number of potential approaches it may generate, and the maturity and diversity of the technical marketplace.

Not all prizes have to be in the multimillions, either. Al-though a big number makes it easy to draw attention to the challenge, more modest awards in the tens of thousands of dollars can work if the topic is noteworthy and the promise of a solution is powerful enough to capture the hearts and minds of the technical and media communities.

It is impossible to overestimate the importance of the marketing component of a successful grand challenge. From the announcement of the challenge to the publicity necessary for promoting the sponsor as a visionary organization, the marketing elevates awareness of the message to a broader target community. Every aspect of a grand challenge has marketing potential—the challenge's societal importance, the selection of judges who can help evaluate proposal submissions, the announcement of the challenge launch and close, and, of course, the ultimate determination of the winner and awarding of the purse.

Crafting the right messaging platform, structuring and implementing the appropriate media strategy, including social media, event-izing certain milestones such as the launch of the grand challenge and the close—these and myriad other "moments" throughout the initiative represent millions of dollars' worth of publicity to the sponsoring CEO and his or her organization.

CEOs interested in sponsoring a grand challenge should start by thinking carefully about what their company stands for. Companies such as NineSigma can then help them develop a short list of potential innovation needs that align with their vision. An early question to consider is whether or not to bring in a partner organization. At this point, the vendor is often asked to create a grand challenge presentation for the company's management team in order to get their buy-in and funding approval. They also start interfacing with the organization's marketing department and begin to identify the appropriate internal team to collaborate with on a successful initiative.

Ideally, a year after embarking on a grand challenge, the sponsor can look back and know that they've effectively put their company center stage within their industry and, in doing so, established their organization as a visionary brand. As far as making a lasting impact goes, what more can a CEO want?

THINK ABOUT:

- Can your innovation team, as currently configured, keep up with the market demands on your organization?
- Have any of your competitors used crowdsourcing and, if so, what was the outcome? Why?
- If you decided to give it a go, what would be the theme of your grand challenge?

CHAPTER

Bridge the Generational Divide

The greater the contrast, the greater the potential.
Great energy only comes from a correspondingly
great tension of opposites.
—Carl Jung

Question: Teaming boomers and millennials—is it possible?
Answer: Not only is it possible, but it's critical to the success of
your efforts to create sustainable innovation for your organization.

In my experience, it is far better to create an inclusive environment when forming your in-house innovation SWAT
team. Your company's innovation ringleader must be generation and function agnostic.

Trouble starts when the innovation team gains the percep-
tion of "the cool kids' club"—or "the usual suspects" as Captain
Renault said in the film classic *Casablanca*.

Key Demographics and the (Fast) Changing of the Workplace Guard

According to US Census statistics, baby boomers and millennials (or gen Y, aged eighteen to thirty-three) are large groups:

there are seventy-seven million boomers and—yes, believe it!—eighty-six million millennials. The relative size of these two groups surprises many savvy business leaders.

2015 Age Pyramid

Age	Men	Women
75 - 79	3.4	4.4
70 - 74	5.0	6.0
65 - 69	7.3	8.3
60 - 54	9.0	9.8
55 - 59	10.5	11.1
50 - 54	11.0	11.4
45 - 49	10.4	10.5
40 - 44	10.1	10.1
35 - 39	10.4	10.2
30 - 34	11.1	10.8
25 - 29	11.3	10.9
20 - 24	11.2	10.7
15 - 19	10.4	9.9
10 - 14	10.7	10.3
05 - 09	11.0	10.6
00 - 04	11.4	10.9

Boomers 51-69 (74M)

Millennials 19-37 (83M)

Source: THCreativity, Inc.

Leading-edge boomers were supposed to be retiring in the next five to ten years. But the instability of the financial markets has proven a factor in the rooting of boomers to the workforce. Many impatient millennials, eager to move forward with their careers, are not happy with this turn of events. However, there are wide-ranging considerations about this eventual brain drain from the workplace.

The US business community is facing a war of intelligence attrition. Fortune 500s will see countless experienced knowledge workers walk out the door over the next two decades.

The US armed forces are losing millions of officers and key personnel to retirement.

For even those companies that thrive on innovation, the numbers are daunting—and demand action. Some 900,000 white-collar workers from the executive branch of government, and another 5,400 federal executives, will be up for retirement over the next decade, according to a study from Tandberg.

A *McKinsey Quarterly* survey found that the baby boomer generation is "the best-educated, most highly skilled aging workforce in US history." Though they're "only" about 40 percent of the workforce, they comprise more than half of all managers and almost half of all professionals, such as doctors and lawyers.

Many are preparing to leave—and American leadership isn't prepared to lose them.

To paraphrase one-time presidential contender Ross Perot, that "*giant sucking sound*" being heard across the business landscape is the vacuum of combined institutional knowledge locked up in the heads of millions of baby boomers heading off into retirement.

Truth be told, in many quarters there is no love lost between these two groups, on either side of the age spectrum. On one side, I hear the demeaning comments about the so-called selfie generation. And what I have heard about the boomers from impatient millennials is far from complimentary.

Millennials: A Snapshot

The millennial generation will make up around 75 percent of the global workforce by 2025—that's going to mean a lot of changes within the workplace as baby boomers and gen Xers step back, and millennials step up.

This is a game changer, and it is my belief that companies that do not take this transformation into consideration and begin to reinvent themselves will hit serious speed bumps before long.

A report on millennials in the global workforce released by Deloitte at Davos in 2013 showed that *70 percent* of these young men and women, tomorrow's future leaders, might "reject" what business—as traditionally organized—offers. Indeed, this group would prefer to work independently through digital means in the future, according to the report.

Millennials, the report further infers, prefer "social enterprises"—places where young talent has the sense that they can influence the future of the business, actively participate in innovation, and create new products and services.

Deloitte's study revealed that globally, 78 percent of millennials are influenced by how innovative a company is when deciding if they want to work there—and believe that innovation is essential for business growth. Yet only 26 percent of millennials feel that business leaders are doing enough to encourage practices that foster innovation.

Further, most say their current employer does not greatly encourage them to think creatively—does not actively encourage and reward intrapreneurship. The millennials surveyed believe the biggest barriers to innovation are management attitude (63 percent) and operational structures and procedures (61 percent). This is a clarion call for today's CEOs.

"A generational shift is taking place in business as boomers, many of whom have been wedded to the 'old way' of doing business, begin to step down from their leadership roles to retire," said Deloitte Global CEO Barry Salzberg. "Real opportunity exists for organizations to step up and create the conditions and commitment needed to encourage innovation in their work environments . . . If we get this right, we can better retain talent, remain more competitive into the future, and more positively impact society," he said.

Adds Olivier Fleurot, CEO of MSL Group, the international strategic communications consultancy, "In the last ten years, young entrepreneurs have successfully and very visibly created their own companies, turning their backs on the traditional workplace. They've demonstrated that going it alone, with a great idea, is a very real alternative to a 9 to 5 today.

"Conversely, traditional companies have had to start competing with these hot start-ups . . . to recruit the diverse talents needed to thrive in today's digital, global era," he said.

What he is saying is that companies that want to survive must reconcile the values of their organization, as currently configured, with the expectations and values of the millennials. "This can only be achieved through 'employee engagement 2.0,'" he said. "This is a reset . . . to engage and re-understand their increasingly millennial employees . . ."

Fight the Brain Drain to Retain Institutional Knowledge

At the same time disaffected millennials accelerate their entry into leadership, management is now faced with seeing their institutional knowledge slip out the door with each successive retirement party.

No matter the frustrations some millennials have with older boomers. Those born between 1946 and 1964 are, in fact, retiring, if not at the speed originally predicted prior to the 2008 economic meltdown. And as they do finally "leave the building," executive leadership faces a daunting task.

The loss of business intelligence and corporate knowledge, especially in R&D-focused companies or organizations, could amount to billions of dollars in lost intellectual capital. Leaders must act fast.

Even those organizations with young employees must consider knowledge management. Knowledge loss also occurs as key personnel resign or are lost to illness or tragedy, taking with them a trove of irreplaceable knowledge.

The question becomes: How do leaders keep the older generation actively engaged so that process of extracting and archiving key information is interesting, challenging, and rewarding?

We have found the following techniques to be effective:

- **Establish and share rules of and rationales for engagement.** Determine how information gathering will be accomplished—for example, by questionnaire, survey, online system, etc. Will salespeople drop into the contact management system such key nuggets as a client's admin's name, or the client's birthday, or his preference to be called Robert, and not Bob, thus strengthening key relationships? If so, be sure to tell the entire organization to do this—and why this should be done.

- **Scan the personnel landscape.** Create a database charting individual or shared "expertise clusters" across the organization. Use relationship software or "spiders" to track knowledge by department and employee. Learn, cross-reference, and document where key knowledge or competencies reside. If a key term or phrase were searched by project or product, specific individuals' names should come up.

- **Set up a database or system for collecting information.** This is especially important in larger organizations. It's not enough to do a knowledge dump from one person to another. Resignation or illness could strike, leaving the company in the same situation again. Create a sustainable "knowledge library" system to capture key data, information, and processes. Database solutions can be as simple as a shared Excel spreadsheet or use of enterprise collaboration platforms such as Confluence (www.atlassian.com/software/confluence), Socialtext (Document7www.socialtext.com), or TWiki (twiki.org). Such systems are easy to create, update, and maintain, and make sharing knowledge across the organization a simple process.

- **Create a home for—and invite—nuanced info.** At my old company, Airspray International, we manufactured screw-on pumps that transformed liquid soap into foam. Early on, clients called about "leakers"—pumps that loosened during shipment. Our president discovered the right amount of "let-off torque" to keep them in place. Because how much torque varied by bottle type, such experience-borne knowledge could not be written in customer instructions. Soon after, he took ill and left the company—but not before writing this key bit of pass-along information in a reference manual used by everyone who's come after him.

- **Build bridges early on.** Like a mentor/apprentice relationship, encourage interaction between the generations. This can foster an esprit de corps and facilitate a transfer of knowledge across ranks and age groups.

- **Host events to bring people together.** Monthly breakfasts, after-work happy hour chats, and other informal exchanges can create opportunities for verbal or hands-on knowledge sharing. Hold a seminar in effective knowledge-sharing principles and practices; invite the entire organization.

- **Use social media and online tools.** Create a closed group on LinkedIn, subscribe to an online whiteboard or collaborative application, create a spreadsheet or chart on Google Docs, set up a blog, forum, or company intranet where retirees can return online and enter insights they recall after leaving the organization. Don't be afraid to crowdsource (there's that word again) new ideas from retirees by sending e-blasts or messages via group tools.

- **Make knowledge sharing a continual, perpetual habit, not a one-time act.** Encourage people to document and share what they know. Invite, even incentivize, retirees to return to share solutions later when they may recall something they've done in the past.

Remember, no tidbit is too small. It's just not about the knowledge behind what they did. Gather details regarding the "work-arounds" they devised and the minutia involving their otherwise undocumented experience of things that work—and things that don't. Even informal practices—like a workflow system that has proven effective—must be put into writing for archival and sharing purposes.

Can't We All Just Get Along?

Older generations of workers are sometimes annoyed and perplexed by millennials, many of whom want to take on big projects and responsibilities right off the bat, whereas earlier generations expected to pay their dues first. Millennials are also adept at communicating across platforms. They tweet, text, and (sometimes) email one another. To non-millennials, it appears to be a nonstop exchange of information and opinions.

"They're so impatient and have such short attention spans" is a typical boomer lament about the millennials they work with.

On the other side of the coin, millennials are increasingly frustrated by boomers who, at best, are seen as selfish (for having lingered in the workplace for so long, taking up those increasingly rare plum spots), IT challenged, and, at worst, believed to be guilty of the ruination of the American dream, the environment, the health-care system, Social Security, and so much more.

There's a little truth and a lot of exaggeration to their arguments—on both sides.

I recently read the tale of one executive who was starting a big IT project. She was shocked and a little embarrassed to learn that her mostly millennial team had identified a lack of support for the effort among higher-ups. How? During her introductory presentation, they sent instant messages among themselves and to others in the company and figured it out.

A thought in the book *Why Nations Fail*, by Daron Acemoglu and James Robinson, may help us shed light on why millennials—in the right environment—are well suited to take innovation to new heights. The authors posit that when a small, closed group of elites holds power, it tends to limit information and education and resist innovations that threaten its strength. By contrast, innovation *thrives* when information is freely available, education is cultivated, people can easily form new groups, and decision making is inclusive rather than exclusive. These circumstances offset the strong tendency of those in power to resist change—in a country or, by extension, at an organization.

In addition, the authors explained how social media saturates every facet of millennials' lives and fosters the type of environment where innovation flourishes. As I've personally seen—and I'm sure you have, as well—they bristle in environments where information is blocked by turf wars, corporate hierarchy, and other forms of organizational constipation. When compared with older generations, millennials learn quickly, and not only want, but need, a free flow of new information, a key driver of innovation.

At some companies, savvy leaders successfully tap into millennials' abilities. For instance, I have observed one senior executive ask younger staff members to introduce the instant messages they constantly send during the meeting directly into the discussion. Rather than keeping the two streams of information separate, he is intentionally encouraging and inviting the parallel conversation into the mix.

I have found that millennials work closely and intensely, have superior right- and left-brain skills, ask great questions, learn fast, take risks, and are fairly altruistic. The folks I've met in business here and abroad are good, solid, family-oriented corporate citizens who want to make a better world—and can use technology to make it happen. But that's been my experience. Let's pursue this further.

Who Are These Millennials? Let's Dig Deeper

"The twenty-three-year-olds I work with are a little over the conversation about how we were the superpower brought low," said Ben Smith, the editor in chief of BuzzFeed, in a recent story in the *New York Times*. "They think that's an 'older person conversation.' They're more interested in this moment of crazy opportunity, with the massive economic and cultural transformation driven by Silicon Valley. And kids feel capable of seizing it. Technology isn't a section in the newspaper anymore. It's the culture."

Ben Domenech, the thirty-two-year-old libertarian who writes the *Transom* newsletter, thinks many millennials are paralyzed by all their choices. He quoted Walker Percy's *The Last Gentleman*: "Lucky is the man who does not secretly believe that every possibility is open to him."

We seem to know so much about the boomers, who are unflatteringly characterized in some quarters as former flower children gone corporate, greedily devouring Earth's precious resources, single-handedly bringing the world's economy to its knees in the late 2000s and sucking the Social Security system dry. Those broad stereotypes are as unfair as those of tattooed, fedora-wearing, Adderall-addled millennials frantically texting, obsessed with the social media platform du jour, while sipping artisanal small-batch bourbon poured by a bearded mixologist in trendy Williamsburg, Brooklyn.

AS MILLENNIALS COME OF AGE

There is much more at play, of course. A fascinating new survey by Pew Research, "Millennials in Adulthood," sheds light on the demographic and psychographic attributes of these young Americans, who are drifting away from traditional institutions. According to the survey and to Pew's analysis:

- "Half of millennials now describe themselves as political independents and 29 percent are not affiliated with any religion—numbers that are at or near the highest levels of political and religious disaffiliation recorded for any generation in the last quarter century."
- "Millennials are the first in the modern era to have higher levels of student loan debt, poverty, and unemployment and lower levels of wealth and personal income than their two immediate predecessor generations had at the same age."
- "Just 26 percent of millennials are married. When they were the age that millennials are now, 36 percent of gen Xers, 48 percent of baby boomers, and 65 percent of the members of the silent generation were married."
- "Asked a longstanding social science survey question, 'Generally speaking, would you say that most people can be trusted or that you can't be too careful in dealing with people?' just 19 percent of millennials say most people can be trusted, compared with 31 percent of gen Xers, 37 percent of silents, and 40 percent of boomers."
- "Millennials are 'digital natives'—the only generation for which the Internet, mobile technology, and social media are not something they've had to adapt to."

Although half of millennials describe themselves as independent, 57 percent say their views on social issues "have become more liberal" over the course of their lives. This is in direct opposition to older generations, who, Pew says, have about half or more of the group saying their social views "have become more conservative." One might argue that millennials simply haven't lived long enough to hit the triggers that might engender

more conservatism—marriage, families, mortgages—
but it could just as well be that this group of young
people is fundamentally different.

Part of the issue for us—as builders of sustainable
innovation—is that millennials seem to shun institutions. Furthermore, millennials were the sole generation in which a majority supported bigger government
with more services as opposed to smaller government
with fewer services.

What is my net takeaway? Based on my experience
working with clients worldwide, I generally see a wave
of liberal-minded, earnest, and hardworking men and
women detached from iconic organizational structures.
Millennials are uniquely prepared for a shifting economy that requires digital competency as well as the ability to acquire new skills. This is a generation in which
institutions play a subordinate role to the individual.
Their social network worlds are digitally generated, not
built brick by brick.

So . . . What Do Millennials *Want*?

The bottom line is that the millennial generation is our future.
If we are to maximize our ability to create sustainable innovation, we must find ways to bridge the generational divide and
encourage these leaders of tomorrow to roll up their proverbial
sleeves and help move the innovation needle.

This requires *all of us* to peel back the layers of truth on
who and what the millennial generation is all about, in order to
attract and retain their copious skills and ironclad work ethic.

First, let's revisit the Deloitte findings referenced earlier
in this chapter. "To attract and retain talent, business needs to

show millennials it is innovative and in tune with their world-view." So said Barry Salzberg, Deloitte's CEO.

By 2025, millennials will comprise 75 percent of the global workforce. A vast majority of these millennials want to work for organizations that foster innovative thinking, develop their skills, and make a positive contribution to society. More than previous generations, millennials are ready to work independently if their needs go unmet by a traditional organization. The businesses up for the challenge of meeting these higher expectations will have the prospect of developing innovative products and services that benefit society while attracting the most talented next-generation workers.

Deloitte's third annual Millennial Survey, referenced earlier, explored what millennials want from business, government, and the future workplace. In fact, this survey gathered the views of more than 7,800 millennials from twenty-six countries who had a college or university degree and who were employed fulltime by organizations of varied sizes.

The report's five key findings were:

1. Business Could Achieve More

Fifty percent of millennials want to work for a business with ethical practices. Millennials believe business can do much more to address society's challenges in the areas of resource scarcity (68 percent), climate change (65 percent), and income inequality (64 percent). Although not fully achieving its potential, millennials still feel business is having a positive impact in areas traditionally seen as the responsibility of government, such as education, skills, training, and health-care/disease prevention.

2. Government Is Not Doing Enough

Millennials believe governments have the greatest capacity to address society's biggest issues but are overwhelmingly failing to do so. Almost half of millennials felt governments were having a negative impact on areas identified as top challenges: unemployment (47 percent), resource scarcity (43 percent), and income inequality (56 percent).

3. Organizations Must Foster Innovative Thinking

Seventy-eight percent of millennials were strongly influenced by how innovative a company was when deciding if they wanted to work there, but most say their current employer does not encourage them to think creatively. Millennials believe the biggest barriers of innovation were management attitude (63 percent), operational structures and procedures (61 percent), and employee skills, attitudes, and diversity (39 percent). Sixty percent of millennials believe organizations can become good at innovation by following established processes, and that innovation can be learned and is repeatable rather than being spontaneous and random. And that's at least some good news for us in the "Ideate. Align. Repeat." camp.

4. Organizations Must Nurture Emerging Leaders

Almost one in four millennials are "asking for a chance" to show their leadership skills. Fifty percent believe their organizations could do more to develop future leaders.

5. Millennials Are Eager to Make a Difference

Millennials believe the success of a business should be measured in terms of more than just financial performance, with a focus on improving society.

According to the report's findings, I find it clear that millennials are looking to business for an innovation-friendly environment—and that they want to contribute and make their mark, or be "impact players" in the sports vernacular. Organizations that foster a culture of innovation will outhustle their competition in retaining tomorrow's top talent and create the next game-changing innovations.

How to Get the Best Millennial Talent

Based on these findings, I believe you will agree that, to compete for the best millennial talent, organizations will have to change. Goldman Sachs, for example, recently announced its intention to improve the work environment of its junior bankers by having them work less, which flies in the face of Wall Street tradition. Typically, newbies often work late, seven days a week, often sleeping and showering in the office.

Goldman made the change partly because it was losing millennials to start-ups. But start-ups typically offer less pay and equally long hours, which suggests that providing more time off isn't the only answer. If corporate cultures don't align with the transparency, free flow of information, and inclusiveness that millennials highly value—and that are also essential for learning and successful innovation—the competitiveness of many established businesses will suffer.

Organizational structure should be reviewed and modified as appropriate. Think about co-working spaces, new desk layouts and floor plans, and a whenever/wherever/however approach to the work environment that, in the right organization, help attract today's younger, lifestyle-focused employees.

According to Tom Agan, a cofounder and the managing partner of Rivia, an innovation and brand consulting firm,

"Millennials are becoming more aware of their rising worth. Coupling their ability to learn quickly with their insistence on having a say, they pack a powerful punch," he said. "But rather than complaining, it's time to embrace millennials for what they can offer, to add experience from older workers to the mix, and to watch innovation explode."

This is optimistic talk and I believe that we, as enablers of innovation, think optimistically. Through workplace corridors, however, I see a general malaise that must be acknowledged and addressed.

Allow me to get up on the soapbox for a quick moment. Here in the US, and around the world, we have decidedly entered very troubling, uncertain times. Here in the US it seems that we're a little bit scared and long for a simpler time (that may or may not have ever existed in the first place).

But here we are, a nation of immigrants, now unable to pass immigration reform despite majority support, or significant infrastructure projects, or myriad pieces of legislation that would spur strength in our now-fragile middle class—arguably the driver of the world's economy.

Andrew Kohut, pollster for Gallup and the Pew Research Center for more than four decades, calls the mood "chronic disillusionment." He said that in this short twenty-first century of ours, we have had only three brief moments when a majority of Americans said they were satisfied with the way things were going: the month W. took office, right after the 9/11 attacks, and the month we invaded Iraq.

The remaining members of the silent generation, many boomers, and even a few gen X members hearken wistfully to the days when, if you work hard and play by the rules, you'll win the day. Now, it's all about whose algorithms are faster, or who can synch up their computers to make bets on Wall Street faster than the next guy.

In such a time, it can be natural—if unwise—to pull in the horns a bit. I think there are a lot of people hungry for a clarity, a simplicity that's going to be hard to find in today's world.

To them I say this: bold is not bad. And I think, or at least believe, that our millennials feel the same way.

Young people are more optimistic than their elders. They are competitive but not players in some death-to-the-vanquished, zero-sum game. They think of themselves, with two feet on the ground and their antennae seeking and finding the good in each successive wave of technological advancement.

Walter Isaacson, head of the Aspen Institute and author of the best-selling *Steve Jobs*, agreed that "there's a striking disconnect between the optimism and swagger of people in the innovative economy—from craft-beer makers to educational reformers to the Uber creators—and the impotence and shrunken stature of our governing institutions."

Nathaniel Philbrick, the author of *Bunker Hill: A City, a Siege, a Revolution*, has said, "They weren't better than us back then; they were trying to figure things out and justify their behavior, kind of like we are now. From the beginning to the end, the Revolution was a messy work in progress. The people we hold up as paragons did not always act nobly but would then later be portrayed as always acting nobly. It reminds you of the dysfunction we're in the middle of now.

"The more we can realize that we're all making it up as we go along and somehow muddling through making ugly mistakes, the better. We're not destined for greatness. We have to earn that greatness. What George Washington did right was to realize how much of what he thought was right was wrong."

End of this soapbox sermon. For now.

How to Create a Millennial-Friendly Workplace

Keep this in mind: in less than a decade, millennials will out-number boomers in the workplace.

This is important, because there is a rift between the two groups that requires careful patching. In fact, the conflict isn't isolated to just boomers and millennials. According to the authors of *Crucial Conversations: Tools for Talking When Stakes Are High* (Kerry Patterson, Joseph Grenny, Ron McMillan and Al Switzler), grumpy boomers also gripe about gen Xers (thirty-four to forty-eight years old) for alleged "lack of discipline and "easy distraction." Gen Xers, for their part, side with the millennials' description of boomers, and yet believe millennials to be arrogant. Millennials believe gen Xers have poor problem-solving skills and are generally slow to respond.

But the main bout seems to be between millennials and boomers, and it is a drain on productivity, according to the aforementioned authors. They write that this sniping and stereotyping is causing one in three of us to waste about five hours a week on intergenerational conflicts. "Learning how to speak up, regardless of age or authority, can resolve conflict and improve productivity in today's multigenerational workplace," the book states, offering these four steps for getting started:

1. Start on the Same Page

Begin with a statement of respect and intent to achieve mutual goals. "We live in a culture where people don't confront each other. It's fight or flight," said the authors. "When we're concerned, we often go to silence and then the problem builds up. When we do speak up, we speak with anger." He advised leaders to speak for thirty seconds at most, and then allow the other person ample time to contribute. More than thirty seconds, and your potential teammate will turn a deaf ear to anything further you have to say.

Remind others that you're not standing between them and their goal. Be obvious about your motive, and ask if you can share your ideas. "Lead from heart, not from head," the book advises.

2. Lead with the Facts

Rather than starting off judgmental about someone's age or your assumptions about why they behaved the way they did, remain neutral in tonality. "Stick to the facts, not that you think the guy is a lazy, disrespectful jerk," the book states. Be specific and explain what you expected to see and what you actually saw, describing the gap.

3. Remain Nonjudgmental and Don't Become Hypercritical

Once you've stated the facts as you see them, you've hit the hazardous half-minute. "You have the first thirty seconds to make your case and turn it from a monologue into a dialogue. If you drone on more than thirty seconds, you're dead," according to the authors. If your colleague becomes defensive, pause and reassure him or her of your positive intentions.

4. Invite a Response

Finally, after sharing your concerns, encourage your colleague to respond and share his or her perspective. Be willing to listen, remembering that you're on the same team.

"Inviting a dialogue will result in greater openness, especially if the person has less authority, power, or age than you do."

Finally, Remember This

No matter which side of the generational divide you're on, remember that while you're in the workplace, you are on the same team, trying to reach the same goal: sustainable innovation.

So, for everyone's sake, take a deep breath, and remember that:

- Millennials are passionate, innovative, collaborative, and results-oriented.
- Millennials have a strong work ethic, but one that is defined differently—they care less about the path to achieving the goal and are red-tape averse.
- Organizations must learn to adapt to their millennial employees to gain access to, and leverage, their energy, drive, and solutions. They require frequent and specific feedback—this is what they're used to. While extremely facile with technology, they need to be shown how to express themselves appropriately in a professional setting—this remains a management function, and a valuable one, at that.
- Millennials, for their part, must adapt as well. They are used to a fast-paced, instant-feedback world. However, not everyone in the workplace is tuned to that frequency. Performance reviews are not going to happen every fifteen minutes. On the other hand, it is unfair to interpret their aspiration as "entitlement." Their technical adroitness should not be confused with "overconfidence."

As I said, we're all in this innovation stew together. And, unmistakably, the future will belong to the millennials. By working together for a smooth transition, and trying to understand the cultural differences that forged the mind-sets of the generations, we can create a scenario where the baton of institutional knowledge accrued by the boomers can be smoothly passed to gen Xers and millennials, to ensure short-term continuity and—ultimately—a rise to new heights of success for us all.

It's not easy, not by a long shot. To quote Jeff Jarvis, author of *What Would Google Do?*: "Life is a beta."

THINK ABOUT:

- What is the split in your office between boomers and millennials? Is the working relationship between the two groups solid or can it use fine-tuning?
- As your boomers retire, what steps are being taken to capture their precious institutional knowledge?
- What are you doing—or what could you be doing—to attract and retain the innovation leaders of tomorrow?
- Millennials: have you done everything possible to understand the elders in your work environment and earn their trust?

CHAPTER 9

Robert's Innovation Roundtable

No matter how well you perform, there's always somebody of intelligent opinion who thinks it's lousy.

—Sir Laurence Olivier

The Art of Innovation Implementation and You

With this second book, *Robert's Rules of Innovation II: The Art of Implementation*, we first quickly revisited our ten key rules of innovation and then dove into hands-on ways to break down the barriers to innovation, whether they are self-imposed or due to external or marketplace reasons.

The goal, of course, is to help you to more easily—and sustainably—implement the ten imperatives designed to help your organization innovate. We explored how to:

- Create an innovation mantra
- Fight the culture of fear
- Master CEO-speak
- Build organizational consensus around innovation
- Build, and pressure test, your innovation team
- Avoid becoming a one-hit wonder

- Crowdsource your way to innovation
- Bridge the generational divide

I hope *Robert's Rules of Innovation II: The Art of Implementation* helps inspire you to take your innovation program to the next level and ensure not only that it is sustainable, but that it is repeatable too. Now, you and your team will be capable of reaching new heights at a time of great challenge and equally great opportunity.

As our roundtable participants say, the commitment must come from the top. Whether incremental or disruptive, innovation is a must. It is not easy: it never is. But it must be done. Some things have not changed since 2010, when our first book came out: *Innovation is a people-oriented endeavor, and people are resistant to change.*

I feel confident that you will push through the wall of resistance and make things happen within your organization. Mastering the art of implementation is not easy. As you've come to understand, it is in fact an "art" rather than a "science" and requires steady (some might say relentless) pressure to mold culture.

But it is certainly worth the time and effort to do it right, as our roundtable participants will agree. It takes leadership, discipline, and more than a bit of swagger to get buy-in from all levels of your organization. It takes, in some instances, sheer force of will.

And here I'll say it again—*it must be done.*

Now, let's visit our innovation roundtable. It is time to provide some final advice and encouragement from my network of business associates in various industries around the world. As in book one, I'll share their comments verbatim, in a lively roundtable, Q&A format.

Today, we have with us:

- **Casper Kleiman**, Innovation Professional, LuxperienceLab
- **Nathalie S. Nowak**, former director of Marketing and Innovation, Albea Group; former group marketing director, Delsey Luggage
- **Costas Papaikonomou**, cofounder of Happen Group
- **Frido Smulders**, associate professor; director of Master Strategic Product Design, Delft University of Technology
- **Nicolas Bry**, senior vice president, Orange Vallée
- **Paul Hobcraft**, advisor on innovation transformation, Ticino, Switzerland, Professional Training & Coaching
- **Dr. Wayne Delker**, senior vice president, chief innovation officer, The Clorox Company
- **Chris Thoen**, senior vice president, global head of Science & Technology, Flavour Division, formerly managing director, Global Open Innovation Office, Global Business Development, P&G
- **Tom Ingvoldstad**, innovation lead, managing director, Inneox.com

I hope you enjoy their insights and candor as much as I did.

Innovation Implementation

Robert Brands: Welcome, all of you. I'd like to start today's roundtable by asking your opinion on this: Given the widespread fixation on quarterly reporting and "making numbers," what is your long-term prognosis for the ability of organizations to create and implement sustainable innovation programs?

Paul Hobcraft: Let me start by stressing that "innovation" is a people-centric activity—people fall in love with processes, but forget the key thing: the person. There are not many books on innovation with "people"—or HR—at its core. And it's not just about physical proximity, but the degree of connectivity and sharing—that's what makes it possible to implement innovation for the long haul.

RB: Paul, how do you tie that back to quarterly-report fixation?

Paul: I see so many companies now that are risk averse and that push predictability. This short-termism makes innovation implementation fated to fail. The push to increase shareholder value forces us to reduce risk.

Chris Thoen: When you compare where we are now, versus 2008, the leash has not gotten longer. Companies still struggle with the residual impact of the Great Recession and are still shell-shocked and less willing to take risks. There is a great dependency on cost cutting as the road to corporate performance. Wall Street sets the tune. But this will be self-correcting, as some brands erode and are replaced by more aggressive companies.

RB: In place of disruptive innovation, what do you see, Chris?

Chris: A lot of companies are perfectly all right with incremental innovation. And then, there is open innovation, which mitigates the risk, as they partner with companies that have done the initial work. The question is: What happens over time when you keep "watering down the whiskey," so to speak?

Wayne Delker: Look, innovation is uncertain, and today, companies don't feel comfortable with uncertainty. For them, it's about portfolio management and creating the right blend of projects.

RB: Wayne, where do you stand on processes such as Stage-Gate?

Wayne: It brought a lot of value to the innovation world. You hire smart people and give them tools to work with. It's a manageable process, but the downside is that it brought with it "incrementally." The upside: you innovate in a way that allows the least amount of waste.

RB: And Six Sigma?

Wayne: Six Sigma reduces variability and improves consistency. It helps take massive amounts of cost out of the system. The question is: for innovation to happen, is this approach a straitjacket? In implementing innovation, variability is a good thing . . .

Casper Kleiman: Yes, there must be something more to company success that is more aspirational, more human. Successful innovation implementation requires a broad-spectrum, coherent vision—a holistic approach, a longer-range view. When you drive your car, you can't just look at the road immediately ahead. It takes a big-picture view.

Paul: Thank heavens there are organizational leaders beginning to push back on the obsessive need for quarterly reporting.

RB: Such as?

Paul: Google, Unilever, Coca-Cola, and National Grid have signaled the end for quarterly reporting. This signals a renewed focus on the longer term. National Grid's CEO recently said that chief executives and investors must move beyond financial value as the only recognized metric of business success. And UL's CEO, Paul Polman, said basically, "If you buy into this long-term value creation model—which is sustainable—then come and invest with us. If you don't, I respect you as a human being, but don't put your money in our company."

Disruptive vs. Incremental Innovation

RB: Let's go back to that term Wayne used a moment ago: "incrementally." What are your thoughts on breakthrough innovations versus incremental advances?

Wayne: One can lose a lot of sleep going for home run after home run. A case can be made for creating a robust pipeline spread over multiple divisions. Keep your core healthy, keep the brand vibrant, and create enough news to generate ongoing retailer excitement.

Costas Papaikonomou: For me, successful innovation is not about dreaming up what would be science fiction today, but about foreseeing what would be plain vanilla tomorrow. This is not about "black magic." Breakthrough ideas often feed creative egos, not consumer needs. If anything, successful new products and services are like the weather.

RB: How so?

Costas: In the sense that they're about 90 percent the same as yesterday's products. And that's not to say the world does not need game changing innovation. It's merely that too many businesses waste time looking outside the box when their market still has plenty of room left to grow and differentiate inside it.

RB: So you don't advocate for going for the big home run, Costas?

Costas: In my opinion, wishful thinking and blue-sky ideation are absolutely fine. But, think of them as a transfer station, not the end destination of the effort. Even the wildest ideas must come back to earth in order to become part of an operational process that can make a business thrive.

Tom Ingvoldstad: I see the "holistic" approach noted by Casper as a way for innovation to help us create dynamic solutions that can serve mankind and solve huge global issues.

RB: Tom, I think you're onto something. Please elaborate.

Tom: From healthcare, to refugees, to water shortages—innovation can help us resolve big issues. For example, a recent Israeli-California business pact will include research facilities and funding to address water scarcity, cyber security, and climate change issues.

In the healthcare arena, disruptive innovation has paired IT professionals and doctors, who are developing a Pillcam, which is a $500 alternative to a $4,000 procedure: the colonoscopy. IKEA and the UN's refugee agency have teamed to create shelters for the displaced citizens of Iraq. It's about harnessing the talents of various groups of people to generate something all new. Disruptive is good. And, yes, it is, in fact, all about the people involved.

At its purest level, innovation forces us to look at a problem holistically. For example, "*Why* do we get sick?" is the question that can open the door to healthcare solutions.

RB: What's the biggest challenge?

Tom: It's up to the decision makers, those at the top of the organizational hierarchy, who guide the process. We humans start out able to see a different future and we are free to act upon our vision. That's innovation. Add too much process, too much control, and innovation is killed. Why put such human potential in that straitjacket?

Ideation and Brainstorming

RB: Let's follow that line of conversation up with your thoughts on the brainstorming—and ideation—processes. What works? What does not work?

Nathalie S. Nowak: It is, in fact, about the people. The right mix of people in the innovation process can spell success. I like to mix various types of people: extroverts, open-minded, environmentally focused, a mix.

Then, while it's important to look at how consumers use your products, it is extremely valuable to look at other industries as well, and see consumer usage patterns, as well as do online research. Of course, innovation for B2B products is very tough, as you must think about the consumer, or end user, as well as convince your customer to buy the product.

Costas: And then you have the renegade innovator, the one that hears "yes" even when the boss says "no." These are people that push their pet product through, by cheating (or "artfully using") the system because they just "know" they're right. They work on a hunch, they can abuse the system, and yet—sometimes you need a guy like that.

RB: It sounds, Costas, as if you're not a proponent of special "brainstorming rooms" and the like?

Costas: You don't need to wear funny hats, play with toys, and sit on beanbag chairs to be creative. You don't need a company retreat to a Hungarian castle. What you need is *time*. Uninterrupted time to work on the task, alone or in a group, to get your head around the problem.

You also need an unfiltered end-user context. Listen to what consumers actually say. Cherish small, incremental ideas.

Frido Smulders: I absolutely agree that we must learn to innovate the innovation process itself. There is such a powerful social dimension to the process. The participants must be well-matched, empowered, and free to fail, and comfortable that this is a long-term, top-down process, not an ad-hoc committee meeting.

RB: Agreed. And I actually think most companies have too many ideas and are not sure of what to do next, how to rank, or prioritize, their findings. For this part of the process, I see a specific, step-by-step approach, starting with idea submission and concluding with comments and input.

Once an idea is submitted and seems to have merit, a new product brief should be created. Typically, this is a custom designed, single-page document with an overview of the idea, a description, info on market size, cost target and sell price, CAPEX needed, and time to develop.

Innovation Implementation: The Buck Stops *Where?*
RB: What is the key to building a top innovation company, with a true culture of innovation?

Nicolas Bry: Without leadership, innovation is governed by budget regulation, committee without inspiration—this will only yield incremental innovation. Without vision and conviction, collaborative innovation ends up as contractual agreement instead of with shared competencies that foster creativity and disruptive, breakthrough innovation.

A Stage-Gate process is important, but it is not a guarantee of success, or for speed. For innovation to step in, meaning must prevail. Product development rules are relevant when they add value. Leadership must work to activate the organization's collective intelligence.

Costas: I totally agree. If the top guys are not onboard, you go nowhere. Top management must all commit to making innovation a key element of the daily business.

RB: I am sensing that you seem to believe that it's people first. Then come the processes—and finally, the ideas.

Nathalie: For me, it is always about the people first. Successful innovation implementation comes down to being an HR-oriented issue.

Chris: Organizational commitment is critical. After that, it all hinges on strategy. Where is your niche? Are you all clear on where you want to be and what you're very good at? Once that is clarified, be daring. Go to adjacencies, the next concentric circle, and extend into that new area. Above all, don't stand still. Today, standing still is falling backwards.

Paul: The innovation buck stops at the top! It will not work in just being "pushed down" the organization. It is the role senior executives must fill to achieve superior innovation success.

If the leadership of the organization fails to formally integrate innovation into the core of the company, innovation results will be disappointing. Leadership needs to explicitly lead and manage and close the gap between aspiration and execution. Leadership must provide the framework, guidance, and direction to make innovation implementation happen.

Rowan: Yes to that and, in addition, I see that although companies are now getting much better at generating new insights and ideas, most of these ideas hit a wall when it comes to the serious allocation of budgets and management talent. They stay stuck in a portfolio of opportunities.

Paul: Sadly, innovation is constantly being driven into the dark corners of the organization. It is treated as opportunistic, like a light bulb you can turn on or off, depending on the need for a big hit.

Innovation needs to be part of overall strategy. Until leadership "leads" by focusing on the longer term, innovation is going to disappoint. Resolution for innovation starts at the top.

THINK ABOUT:

- Does your top management remain involved in your organization's innovation efforts?
- Is your innovation intertwined with corporate strategy, or is it "orphaned" and off to the side?
- Is your organization's innovation effort more of the "incremental" or "disruptive" type? Is that what you prefer? If not, what can you do to turn things around?

- Do you find your ideation sessions productive? Are you comfortable in the format and tonality of these all-important meetings?
- In your group meetings, do you feel you have the optimal mix of participants?

Today we stand on the shoulders of giants in a rapidly changing world. In order to gain the competitive edge needed to stay relevant in today's marketplace, it is imperative that businesses continue to innovate. Without a doubt, innovation is the number one lever to create growth.

Admittedly, it is not easy. But sustainable innovation must be encoded into your corporate DNA. Start with the ten imperatives of Robert's Rules of Innovation. Address the challenges of the art of implementation and tackle them head on. Make innovation part of your organization's monthly routine, NPD meetings, ideation, communications, reward system—every facet of its operations.

You know, in your heart, it must be done. **Innovate and thrive!**

Key Resources and Links

Within these pages, I have referenced a number of companies and services that specialize in helping companies build powerful cultures of sustainable innovation. For your convenience, I have listed them here.

www.robertsrulesofinnovation.com
www.innovationcoach.com
www.innovationexcellence.com
www.brightidea.com
www.commstratpr.com
www.happen.com
www.hoffmannbaron.com
www.ideaslaboratory.com
www.inneox.com
www.improveSF.org
www.ketchum.com
www.paul4innovating.com
www.rapidinnovation.fr
www.socialtext.com
www.stage-gate.com
www.vistage.com
www.wazoku.com

tudelft.academia.edu/FridoSmulders
www.atlassian.com/software/confluence
www.pewresearch.org/topics/millennials
www2.deloitte.com/global/en/pages/about-deloitte/articles/
world-economic-forum-meeting.html
www.innovationmanagement.se/2011/04/21/procter-and-
gambles-chris-thoen-on-open-innovation
ieondemand.com/divisions/Innovation/presentations/innova-
tion-machine-ny

Acknowledgments

The initial idea to share the innovation life learnings of the original *Robert's Rules of Innovation* came six years ago out of discussions with my longtime supporter and friend Marty Kleinman. His ongoing support, skill, and shared enthusiasm have now resulted in our second collaboration, *Robert's Rules of Innovation II: The Art of Implementation*. Once again, his abilities helped make this book possible. A sincere and appreciated *thank-you*.

I also want to acknowledge the hard work of Shana Dysert. Shana has been coauthoring my innovation blogs for more than a year. Her intelligence, enthusiasm, and broad knowledge were integral to the fine-tuning of this book.

This book was completed with full recognition of the contributions made by my friends and coworkers through the years (especially at Airspray), as well as mentors and global leaders in innovation who have helped and inspired me over the years to help me develop into what I have become. Without those who had confidence in me and empowered me to do what had to be done, the success stories would not have followed.

Finally, I want to express my gratefulness for the love and support of my wife, Janice. With her partnership, our life dreams have become reality.

About the Authors

ROBERT F. BRANDS

Robert F. Brands is president and founder of Innovation Coach® (www.InnovationCoach.com) and Brands & Company, LLC.

Brands's hands-on experience in bringing innovation to market spans decades and includes the creation and improvement of product development processes and company culture. He has delivered on his pledge to bring "at least one new product per year to market"—resulting in double digit profitable growth and shareholder value.

He has led worldwide teams responsible for marketing and sales, operations, and R&D and is a regular contributor to real- and virtual-world media and social networking platforms. He is currently a serial entrepreneur and continues to be engaged in business development and start-up companies.

A native of The Netherlands, Brands earned a bachelor of science in Business Administration from HTS Eindhoven. A past (ten-year) Vistage member, past member of Tulane University's and current member of the University of Miami President's Parent Council, and board member of The Netherlands Chamber of Commerce in the United States, Brands is also an avid sailor, open-water diver, and licensed pilot of single-engine aircraft. He resides in Stuart, Florida.

For more information, visit www.linkedin.com/in/ robertfbrands.

MARTIN KLEINMAN

Martin Kleinman is Managing Director of Communications Strategies, LLC, and is a New York–based business writer and communications specialist (www.commstratpr.com). In addition, he blogs for the *Huffington Post*, as well as www.therealnewyorkers.com, and recently published a collection of short fiction, *Home Front*.

Martin holds a BA degree in Economics and Psychology from City University of New York at Lehman College. Martin, who enjoys tennis and cycling, resides in New York City. For more information, visit www.linkedin.com/in/martinkleinman.

Index